# Juiced up!

500 juicing recipes to start juicing for weight loss, juicing for health, and doing a natural juice cleanse on a juice diet

By:
Albert Pino
and
Frank Harris aka "Fat Loss Frankie"

## Legal notice

# Table of Contents

11

15

16

17

# What exactly does "juicing" mean"?

When you make a juice, you are squeezing all (or as much as possible) of the juice out of the produce you are using and you are discarding the insoluble fiber (also known as "pulp"). The juice is the water and typically almost all of the nutrients that naturally occur in the fruit or vegetable.

Juicing is a different process than simply blending some fresh fruits and vegetables in a blender. When you blend produce, the pulp is not extracted and discarded the way it is in a juicer. Instead it is ground of and remains inside of the drink. This adds a more robust texture to your drink that some people like and some people do not. Whether you wish to juice or blend is really a matter of personal preference as far as taste is concerned.

There is a benefit to juicing however that you don't get when you blend. When you removed the insoluble fiber from the produce when you juice it, you do not ingest it when you consume the drink. This makes it much easier for your body to absorb all of the nutrients, enzymes, and antioxidants that naturally occur in the fruits and vegetables you are juicing with. Essentially, juicing provides a faster way for your body to get access to the nutrients it wants.

Juicing is a great way for anyone to consume their daily produce needs. It is an especially good method however, for people who are sick, tired, suffering from an autoimmune condition, or are part of a vulnerable group such as the elderly to get the nutrients they need into their system without any added resistance.

Juicing can also be used as a way to fast. Doing a juice fast means that you are only drinking juice and not eating anything. This is sometimes also referred to as a "juice cleanse". If you are planning on doing a juice fast, especially one that will last for a period of multiple days, weeks, or even months, it is important that you speak to your family doctor before beginning as it is not safe for everyone to abstain from food completely. For people who can do a juice fast safely, the most notable benefit is weight loss. It is possible to achieve truly dramatic weight loss in a very short period of time while doing a juice fast. Most overweight people can expect to lose about one and a half to two pounds *per day* when doing a juice fast. And because juices, especially those containing entirely or primarily vegetables, are so nutritious you can still get the important vitamins and minerals your body needs even without eating food. Many people find doing a "juice cleanse" for a few days once every two to three months is an effective way to maintain a healthy weight and feel re-energized. Juice fasting may seem somewhat extreme but for many people it is both healthier and easier to stick to then any other diet that can cause the same level of fat loss. Part of the success of juice fasting is simply due to the many great tasting juices you can easily make in your own kitchen in just a few minutes! When losing weight is easy and tasty you are much more likely to follow through with it. If you are doing a juice cleanse, and you've checked with your doctor to make sure it is safe for you to do so, you can use any of the recipes in this book for your cleanse. Just make sure that you mostly stick to the recipes that contain mostly or entirely vegetables and limit your consumption of primarily fruit based juices.

# Purchasing a juicer

If you are considering juicing at home, you will require a juicer. Juicers vary widely in terms of their features, speed, power, and cost. One of the first things you will need to decide is whether you want to purchase a centrifugal juicer or a masticating juicer.

## *Centrifugal vs masticating juicers*

Centrifugal juicers tend to be less expensive than masticating juicers. Part of the trade-off in the cost savings is that these juicers are often louder and less efficient in their juicing. The way these juicers work is by spinning the produce at a high speed while grinding it to a pulp. The centrifugal juicer's spinning motion then forces the juice away from the produce as it spins. In this regard, the operation of a centrifugal juicer is somewhat similar to that of a salad spinner: the liquid is separated from the solid by centrifugal force.

The more expensive masticating juicer has a few benefits over the cheaper centrifugal juicers. First of all, it is more versatile. In addition to juicing, you can use a masticating juicer to produce a surprising variety of other goods including baby food, sauces, ice cream, butter, and pasta!

Another key benefit of a masticating juicer is their superiority at juicing dark leafy green vegetables. Centrifugal juicers sometimes struggle to extract all of the juice from dark leafy greens like kale.

The masticating juicers do not use a spinning motion, which makes them quite a bit quieter. They operate instead at a low and consistent speed. Not only does this reduce the noise that the machine produces but it also reduces the heat. This is important because the heat in centrifugal juicers can kill some of the enzymes in your juice, making it less healthy than juice produced with a masticating juicer.

# Sugar consumption

One thing you need to be mindful of when juicing is the sugar content of your juice. Fructose, the primary sugar in fruit juice, is not your friend. Studies have linked fructose consumption to conditions like insulin resistance, weight gain, and heart disease. Excessive consumption of fructose can be harmful in any form, but it is especially harmful when it is consumed in juice rather than whole fruit. This is because when the insoluble fiber has been extracted from the produce, there is nothing to "cushion the blow" of the sugar hitting your stomach and being absorbed into your bloodstream. Just as the body receives an accelerated dose of nutrients and enzymes when you consume juice, it also receives an accelerated dose of fructose!

In addition to the more rapid consumption of fructose contained in juice, there is another potential danger in juicing that could cause you to consume much more sugar than you intend to. When you juice, you consume many more fruits and vegetables than you would have consumed had you eaten them instead. Just a small glass of fruit juice might contain more fruit than you would eat over the course of an entire day.

In this sense, juicing can be a "double edged sword", in that not only does it facilitate easy consumption and absorption of large quantities of beneficial nutrients and enzymes, but it also facilitates the easy consumption and absorption of excessive amounts of harmful fructose!

For this reason, you should favor vegetables as the primary ingredients in your juice. You can then add a much smaller quantity of fruit, preferably relatively low-sugar fruit such as an apple, to sweeten the juice and enhance it's flavor.

# Before you juice

## *Cleaning your fruits and vegetables*

The first thing you will want to do is wash and prep all of the fruits and vegetables that you will be including in your juice. At the very least, you will want to rinse the fruits and vegetables with cold tap water and rub dry with a clean cloth or towel. This is the quickest way to clean your fruits and vegetables, and many people choose to do only this for that reason. Realize though that you are not killing potentially harmful bacteria if you only rinse your fruits and vegetables with tap water. For this reason, this is not a recommended method to employ for cleaning your fruits and vegetables. If you just can't be bothered to do anything more to clean your produce, this is still better than nothing. Just make sure you don't use hot water so the water doesn't have to run through your hot water tank and heater, and let the tap run for a minute or two so that anything that has built up inside the tap or pipes is washed down the drain and not left on your fruits and vegetables.

A better method to prepare your produce for juicing is to use either distilled water or a diluted vinegar solution consisting of one part vinegar and three parts water. If you are juicing frequently, you may find it easier to store your rinsing solution, whether it is distilled water or diluted vinegar, in a spray bottle. Simply spray the produce and rub dry with a clean cloth or towel.

If you don't want to make your own solution, you can purchase a pre-made produce cleaner. There are many commercially available produce cleaners available online and in grocery stores and other major retailers. You will of course pay much more for these solutions than it would cost to simply make a cleaner that is just as effective on your own.

## *Cleaning your juicer*

In order to prevent mold and other harmful bacteria from making its way into your juice, it is important that you keep your juicer clean. If you haven't used your juicer for awhile, you should clean it before juicing. If you juice every day, it isn't necessary to clean your juicer before you use it as long as you clean it thoroughly after every use. This is actually the best way to clean your juicer as it is much faster and easier to clean your juicer immediately after use.

To clean your juicer, disassemble the removable parts and wash with warm soapy water and a soft cloth or sponge. Some parts of a juicer are typically dishwasher safe. The cover, the pulp container, and the bowl portion of a centrifugal juicer are all usually safe to wash in a dishwasher. Consult your juicer's owners manual to be sure.

## How to use the extracted pulp

If you've juiced before you already know how much pulp is extracted from the fruits and vegetables you use in the juicing process. If you haven't juiced yet, you'll find this out very soon. Many people wonder what they can do with the pulp that is extracted after juicing. Throwing it away seems like such a waste! Fortunately there are a number of options that will allow you to get some extra use out of the extracted pulp other than just throwing it away.

One option is to simply use it in your home compost.

Pulp from some vegetables, carrots for example, could also be used to make delicious baked goods such as cake or muffins.

Another option is to use your vegetable pulp to make a delicious vegetable broth. You can easily make a broth by simmering pulp from your favorite vegetables in a pot with some onions, herbs, and water for 30 minutes. Strain when it is done and you have a tasty broth!

# Juice Recipes

The recipes in this book are meant to serve varying numbers of people, but all are meant to serve at least one or two people. We encourage you to experiment with your favorites to get the quantity of juice that you want for you and your family or friends.

If you are using a masticating juicer, you can make larger batches of juice and store the extra juice in an air tight container in your refrigerator for up to three days. Citrus juices can be stored the longest without losing their flavor, but the longer you store any juice the more the nutrients will be lost. If you are juicing with a centrifugal juicer your juice will not last as long due to the additional oxidation that occurs as a result of the high speed spinning. You should consume the juice you make with a centrifugal juicer within 12 hours.

You'll notice as you go through the juicing recipes below that the recipes contain lists of ingredients and information about the nutrition and health benefits of the juice, as well as any drawbacks such as excessive sugar content. What each recipe does not include is specific instructions about mixing and juicing the ingredients. This is because the process doesn't really change from one recipe to another. You simply insert the ingredients into your juicer and the juicer produces your juice!

# Heart Healthy Beet Juice

One beetroot
One medium sized apple
Five medium sized carrots
Half a lemon
Two large peeled oranges

Moderate, consistent carrot consumption has been shown in studies to reduce cholesterol level by about 10 percent. High cholesterol is a leading cause of heart disease, therefore carrot consumption promotes heart health by reducing your risk of heart disease. Consuming carrots regularly also reduces your risk of a heart attack. In fact, some studies show a dramatic decrease in heart attack risk when carrot consumption is maintained over the course of a year. Drinking this juice daily will could lower your risk of a heart attack by up to two thirds!

# Lean Green Machine

One medium sized green bell pepper
One large cucumber
Two cups of spinach
Two medium sized green apples
Three medium sized carrots
Twenty grapes, any variety you like
One medium sized tomato

This is a great juice for boosting your immune system, lowering your blood pressure, and losing weight. The high levels of potassium and magnesium in this juice, as well as the two cups of spinach, work together to lower elevated blood pressure. The juice from the green bell pepper contains powerful antioxidants that contribute to a reduction in cholesterol.

Some people find this drink isn't sweet enough for them. If you like it a little sweeter, simply double or even triple the number of grapes and use a slightly smaller cucumber instead.

# Kale-aid

One large cucumber
Six leaves of kale
Two medium sized apples
Two cups of spinach
One lemon

This is a new healthy spin on a classic refreshing summer favorite, lemonade. And best of all, instead of being loaded with refined sugar like most commercial lemonades available at the grocery store, this juice is great for weight loss while still quenching your thirst with a delicious taste. It contains a significant amount of raw kale. Kale is considered a "super food" and is ideal for weight loss due to its high concentration of nutrients and low calorie content. It is among the most nutrient-dense vegetables available and this juice makes sure you can easily consume this amazing vegetable daily. Kale is also a significant source of organo-sulfur compounds. Studies show these compounds are effective at fighting many different types of cancer. One of the many amazing qualities of kale is that it can actually contribute to a destruction of cancer cells within the body.

In addition to fighting cancer that already exists in the body, kale has also been shown to prevent cancer from occurring in the first place. The sulforaphane contents of kale has been shown to reduce the risk of cancer from occurring in the body.

In addition to the cancer fighting and preventing power of kale, this drink also contains spinach, which is another vegetable studies have shown to be effective in fighting and preventing various types of cancer. The powerful anti-oxidants contained in this vegetable contribute to the deceleration of cancerous cell production and division.

# Cabbage Delight

One quarter of a small head of red cabbage
Three medium sized red apples (Gala, Macintosh, etc.)
Two cloves of garlic
One cup of spinach
One thumb sized piece of ginger root
Five medium sized carrots
One lemon

If you're looking for a way to incorporate more cabbage into your diet but you aren't a big fan of the taste, this juice could be the answer you've been waiting for. This is also a great juice if you're looking to sooth any digestive issues you may be experiencing. The natural laxative in apples can aid with constipation and promote regular bowel movements. The carrots work to cleanse the liver while stimulating a release of bile that is a key component of proper digestions. Juicing with lemon and ginger root not only adds a kick to the juice's flavor, but they also both aid in digestion by reducing gas buildup. Finally, the spinach works to cleanse the intestinal tract while promoting proper digestion.

# Feeling Mint

One large orange
Two apples, any variety
One cucumber
One lemon, peeled
Two cups of mint leaves

This is a great pre-workout beverage as it has just enough sugar in the oranges to get you energized, but not so much that you'll endure a sudden post-sugar crash. The generous helping of mint adds a unique kick to the flavor of this juice that compliments the other fruits and vegetables very well. Mint also delivers some surprising health benefits. Mint has antimicrobial properties and has also been shown to sooth a queasy stomach.

# Strawberry Carrot

Eight medium sized carrots
One and a half cups of strawberries
One medium sized apple
One quarter of a lemon, peeled

This is a filling juice that provides a delicious way to get all the benefits of carrots while masking their flavor with the sweet taste of strawberries. The combination of carrots and strawberries is a favorite flavor of many people who juice regularly. In terms of health benefits, this juice provides a powerful boost to the immune system. The carrots boost the production and efficiency of the white blood cells, which help to defend the body against a variety of infections. The high vitamin C content of the strawberries aid the body in fighting and preventing colds and the flu.

# Life is a Peach

Eight medium sized carrots (or six large carrots)
Three medium sized apples
One medium sized orange
Three large peaches
Half a lemon, peeled

Don't be fooled by all the carrots you're juicing, the end result of this recipe is a smooth, sweet, peachy drink perfect for relaxing outside on a nice summer day. Even if you dislike the taste of carrots, it is important to consume them regularly. Regular carrot consumption has been shown to reduce "bad" LDL cholesterol levels by about 10 percent. High cholesterol is a leading cause of heart disease, therefore carrot consumption promotes heart health by reducing your risk of heart disease and also reducing your risk of a heart attack. This juice can radically improve your heart health while still tasting like a dream.

# Apple Celebration

Four medium sized apples
Three large stalks of celery
One large orange, peeled
One thumbnail sized piece of ginger root

Think of this juice as a new healthier twist on traditional apple juice. The celery, although perhaps not the tastiest produce, is high in vitamins and minerals that help to maintain the skin's youthful elasticity and aid complexion. Celery can also help to calm the nerves and reduce high blood pressure. The orange juice also helps to protect the skin by attacking and eliminating free radicals within the body.

# Greener Pasture

Two medium sized green apples (i.e. Granny Smith)
One medium sized cucumber
Two cups of parsley
One cup of spinach
One half of a lime, peeled

This juice is great for cleansing the body of toxins and facilitating enhanced liver and kidney function. The significant quantity of parsley also makes this juice a powerful immune system booster. Parsley has been shown to promote a strong immune system that keeps the whole body healthy and wards of colds, the flu, and other common ailments. Parsley is nutrient dense and provides a significant source of numerous vitamins including vitamin A, vitamin B 12, vitamin C, and vitamin K.

# Citrus Smash

Four stalks of celery
One peeled lemon
Three medium sized Granny Smith apples (granny smith)
One medium sized pear, any variety you like
Four cups of spinach
Three leaves of kale

This juice has a bold flavor that is all its own, with the sour lemon and sweet apple packing the most punch. Even if you are not a fan of the taste of kale, you will probably still like this juice as the taste is masked by the other ingredients. This is a great juice for improving your complexion and making you feel and look vibrant and youthful. The juice from the lemon functions as a natural antiseptic that promotes skin health. The sodium in the celery is jam-packed with minerals and vitamins which promote elasticity and youthful tightness in the skin. Between the apples and the kale, you're also consuming significant quantities of vitamins A, C, E, and K, all of which prevent the appearance of premature aging by reducing free radicals in the body.

# Mango Morning Zinger

One large mango, peeled (or two smaller sized mangos)
One large orange, peeled
Half a lemon, unpeeled
Two medium sized apples
Cayenne pepper (to taste, start with one pinch)

This juice will wake you up and get you moving with it's fresh
mango flavor and cayenne pepper kick! It also gives you a
substantial dose of vitamins A, B, C, E, K, folate, niacin,
riboflavin, calcium, and iron. A great way to start your day!

# Tropical Treat

One third of a watermelon, rind removed
One third of a pineapple, rind removed
Six strawberries
One cup of blueberries
Half a lime, peeled

This juice is consistently a favorite for it's sweet, delicious taste. Unfortunately this sweet taste comes with a relatively high amount of sugar, meaning this juice really is more of a "treat" than something you would want to enjoy daily. Despite the sugar, the juice still has many health benefits, such as being rich in antioxidants due to the strawberries and blueberries. This juice is a great way to treat yourself without feeling too guilty.

# Summer Sunset

Half a medium sized pineapple
Two large carrots
One large stalk of celery
Half of one lemon, peeled
One glove of garlic

Although it is named after a rich summer sunset, the sweet flavor of this juice means you'll love drinking it at any time of the day or year. And it is not just the taste that makes this juice a popular favorite. The carrots in this juice promote a healthy cleanse by functioning as a diuretic and forcing excess fluid out of the body. In addition, the pineapple is rich in vitamins B6 and C, folate, beta carotene, and thiamin. This juice is a great way to ensure you get the recommended daily dose of potassium, magnesium, and copper. The pineapples and carrots also promote good heart health and can reduce the risk of heart disease.

# Captain Blackberry

One and a half cups of blackberries
Two kiwi
One quarter pineapple
One medium sized pear
Five leaves of peppermint

A smooth juice with just a hint of sour, this juice is always a hit with those who love the taste of blackberries. Pear juice contains high levels of antioxidants, as does the kiwi juice due to it's high levels of copper, iron, and vitamins C and E. The anti-oxidant power of this juice provides a boost to your immune system that can help the body to prevent or quickly fight off colds or the flu.

# Root Root Root for the Home Team

Eight large carrots (or twelve medium carrots)
One beetroot
One yam (sweet potato)

This juice is full of root vegetables that deliver a robust cleanse with a creamy, earthy flavor. Beet juice greatly reduces toxicity of the liver and improves conditions like hepatitis, food poisoning, diarrhea, vomiting, and jaundice. It is a great "reset" for your body after consuming alcohol as it cleanses the liver of the toxic alcohol it has been working to remove from your body. In addition to the cleansing power of beets, the carrots in this juice aid in the cleanse by functioning as a diuretic and forcing excess fluid out of the body.

Beets don't just cleanse the liver though, they also help to cleanse the blood, colon, and gall bladder. Within the bloodstream, the high iron content works to rebuild your red blood cell count so that your body can benefit from increased access to oxygen. In addition, the liver aids in the metabolization of fat. Keeping your liver cleansed and running efficiently promotes weight loss efficiency.

# Natural Anti-inflammatory

Three medium sized carrots
One large orange
Three large stalks of celery
Two thumbnail sized piece of turmeric
One thumbnail sized piece of ginger
Half of one lemon, unpeeled

Studies have widely recognized curcumin, a component of turmeric, as a powerful anti-inflammatory agent. In fact, turmeric contains at least five other components that also have anti-inflammatory effects. Further, more recent studies indicate strong evidence that turmeric also has anti-cancer properties. Despite this, our typical diets don't contain nearly enough turmeric! Juicing with turmeric is a convenient and delicious way to make sure you avail yourself of its many health benefits.

# Cocopeach

One medium sized coconut (scoop the meat out and discard the shell)
One large oranges
Four medium sized peaches

This tasty tropical juice boasts big quantities of copper, iron, potassium, phosphorus, magnesium, zinc, and selenium. These minerals are important for a variety of important functions within the body. Copper and iron work together to improve the flow of oxygen through the bloodstream by boosting the production of red and white blood cells. Selenium contributes to the proper function of the immune system as well as the reproductive system. Magnesium promotes a healthy bone density and together with zinc helps the body to process the macronutrients we consume and turn them into energy the body can use.

# Guava Superjuice

Two medium sized guava, or one large guava (peeled or unpeeled according to preference)
One ruby red grapefruit
One kiwi
One medium sized apple, any variety

Guava is not a popular fruit in many Western countries, which is really unfortunate for us! Guava is a delicious "super fruit" widely consumed in some tropical countries. It earned its reputation as a super fruit due to its high concentration of a wide variety of nutrients and its many health benefits. Among other vitamins, minerals, and nutrients, Guava is particularly rich in copper, vitamin C, lycopene, and antioxidants. If you aren't able to find guava at your local chain grocery store then try a smaller produce market, especially one that carries a variety of ethnic foods.

# The Libido Booster

Three large carrots
Two medium sized Granny Smith apples
One handful of parsley
Two stalks of celery
Five stalks of asparagus
One medium sized stalk of broccoli
One medium sized cucumber
Two table spoons of extra virgin olive oil (stir in after juicing)

Don't let the mild taste of this juice fool you, this recipe delivers a
high powered boost to your libido in an otherwise subtle and
unassuming juice. Studies have shown that a lack of histamines in
the body can cause difficulty reaching orgasm and a lack of
interest in sex. The juiced asparagus stalks are a great source of
folic acid which promotes the production of libido-enhancing
histamines. Parsley has also been shown to improve blood flow
which can enhance sexual stimulation.

# The Morning After

One beetroot
Three cups of spinach
One teaspoon of dried spirulina
Two large stalks of celery

This juice is a great choice after a weekend of indulging in alcohol. The beets in this juice works to reduce alcohol toxicity in the liver and promotes recovery by cleansing the blood and aiding in the delivering of oxygen via the bloodstream. The spinach also has cleansing properties and aids the restoration of the body's circulatory system. It has also been shown to promote brain health, which can help you recover from the mental fog a hang over faster. Finally, the calcium and magnesium in the celery stalks have been shown to ease agitation of the central nervous system.

# Winter Beeter

One beetroot
One medium sized apple
Ten medium sized carrots
Four cups of spinach
One large celery stalk
One cup of raspberries

If you don't like the taste of beets, this may not be the juice for you (although you could always sweeten it up with an extra apple if you want to). Like the other beetroot heavy juices in this book, this one is another great internal cleanse. The beet juice reduces toxicity in the liver which can deliver fast relief from accidental food poisoning, diarrhea, and vomiting. It is also an excellent cure for a hangover due to the liver cleansing beetroot in the juice.

In addition to the beetroot, the apple (or apples) you use in this juice contain a natural laxative. Apple juice facilitates regular bowel movements which add to the cleansing power of this juice.

# Pretty in Pink

One beetroot
One large carrot
Two medium sized apples
One medium sized yam (sweet potato)
One large orange, peeled

This juice packs a sweet flavor in a vibrant pink liquid. The appearance is sure to impress friends with whom you'll want to share this healthy and delicious recipe. Like it's bright pink color, this juice will make you feel vibrant and energized. The beetroot is a great source of fast energy as your body can quickly digest the carbohydrates in the beetroot and use them to fuel your body throughout the day.

This juice also facilitates proper digestion within the body and can aid indigestion. This is due to the natural laxative properties of apples. The juice in the apple promotes regular bowel movements. Carrots and beets also promote regular bowel movements by cleansing the liver and stimulating additional bile release which can aid constipation.

# The Deep Cleanse

One beetroot
One large sized apple, or two smaller sized apples (any variety
you like)
One large stalk of celery
Five medium sized carrots
Thumbnail sized portion of ginger
Half a peeled lemon

When it comes to cleansing, this juice is hard to "beet". The root
vegetables in this juice detoxify the liver, strengthen the blood,
and aid with the reduction of any condition related to toxicity in
the body, such as hepatitis, food poisoning, jaundice, and a hang
over. While cleansing the body, this juice also provides an
immediate energy boost that can last for hours. You can add more
lemon, ginger, or apples if you want to tweak the taste and reduce
the earthy beet flavor.

# Mango Cantaloupe

Half a medium sized cantaloupe
Two peeled mangos
Ten leaves of peppermint

This is a great tasting juice that is best enjoyed in moderation due to the sugar content and the relative lack of health benefits compared to most of the other juices in this book. Despite its status as more of a "dessert juice" it still manages to contain high levels of potassium as well as vitamins A and C. This can make it a good choice for warding off a cold or flu, as well as maintaining or improving the health of your skin, eyes, and immune system.

# Papaya and Peach

Two papaya
Two peaches
One medium sized apple, any variety
One clove of garlic
Thumbnail sized piece of ginger

This is a tasty and exotic juice that makes for a good source of
vitamins A and C. It also contains plenty of antioxidants and
potassium. Try swapping out your plain old morning orange juice
for this and get your day started right.

# The Turmeric Cold Killer

Eight thumb sized pieces or turmeric
Three medium sized carrots
Three medium sized apples
Three large celery stalks
Three medium sized pears
One thumbnail sized piece of ginger
Two peeled lemons

With all of the apples and pears, this juice is a little heavy on the sugar and as such it is not the best choice for a daily juice aimed at promoting weight loss. It is however a powerful cold, flu, and fever remedy that works quickly to boost the body's immune system and fight off illness. If you are suffering from a fever in particular, consider doubling the quantity of ginger you are juicing. The heavy lemon content in this juice facilitates perspiration while reducing feelings of nausea or dizziness. This juice also contains many pears which are great for preventing a cold or flu or fighting one off by fortifying the body's immune system.

# Ginger Stingray

One medium sized stalk of celery
One medium sized cucumber
One medium sized apple, any variety
Half of one lemon, peeled
Half of one lime, peeled
One cup of spinach
Two thumbnail sized pieces of ginger
One clove of garlic

Ginger isn't a flavor for everyone, but those who like it will definitely want to give this juice a try. Even those who do not like the taste of ginger may still appreciate this juice for it's effect on the digestive system. Ginger has been shown to ease digestive issues such as nausea, dizziness, motion sickness, vomiting, or an upset stomach. In fact, studies have shown that ginger is actually superior to popular prescription medication when it comes to providing relief for digestive problems!

# Juice for Sight

Ten medium sized carrots
One large cucumber
One handful of cilantro
One thumbnail sized piece of ginger root
Half a lemon
Half a lime
One dash of cayenne pepper (stirred in after juicing)

This carrot heavy juice is a great way to improve your eyesight and prevent certain diseases that effect the eye. Studies have shown that a deficiency in vitamin A can impair the ability to see in dim light. This juice contains approximately 500% of the required daily dose of vitamin A which makes it ideal for boosting this crucial vitamin in those who may be deficient. The beta-carotene in this juice is also an effective way to prevent macular degeneration, a common condition that impairs sight as the body ages. Studies have shown that people who consistently consume large quantities of beta-carotene can cut their risk of macular degeneration in half.

# Kale Power

Five leaves of kale
One cup of collard greens
One medium sized red bell pepper
One medium sized apple (any variety you like)
Two handfuls of cilantro
Five medium sized carrots

In addition to promoting overall bodily health, this juice can be an effective cancer deterrent. The collard greens are rich in nutrients that have powerful cancer fighting properties. Studies have shown both kale and collard greens can be beneficial at fighting and preventing breast cancer, prostate cancer, colon cancer, and other cancers.

This juice is also a great juice for weight loss. The kale leaves and collard greens are extremely nutrient-dense, meaning they add very few calories to this juice while still managing to deliver a significant quantity of nutrients and anti-oxidants.

# Sweet Broccoli

One cup of broccoli florets
Three medium sized apples
Half a lemon, peeled

Most of us don't eat enough broccoli, which is unfortunate because this vegetable contains high levels of vitamins B, C, and K, as well as several important minerals. Broccoli is "nutrient dense" meaning that it is very low in calories while still being high in a variety of nutrients. Juicing with broccoli has been shown to help prevent the deterioration of eye sight due to age-related conditions like macular degeneration.

Broccoli is also a powerful cleanser and detoxifier. Some of the nutrients contained in broccoli (such as glucoraphanin, gluconasturtiin, and glucobrassicin) facilitate a natural detoxification process in the body by working to activate, neutralize, and eliminate a variety of harmful contaminants.

# Citrus Mint

One large pink grapefruit
One clementine (or substitute for a small orange, or half a large orange)
Half a cup of mint
Two cloves of garlic

This is a simple juice recipe that is easy to whip up first thing in the morning to enjoy with breakfast. It's a great way to get the day started right with a high dose of vitamin C and antioxidants to energize and strengthen the immune system. This juice is also surprisingly filling due to the grapefruit content, which makes it a great choice for a juice fast or weight loss regimen.

# Green Apple Mint

Four Granny Smith apples
Three large celery stalks
One and a half cups of mint leaves
One cup of spinach
One small lime (or half of one large lime), peeled
One quarter of a lemon, peeled

Studies have shown that consuming the juices from apples and lemons can reduce breathing difficulties, improve oxygen intake, and even prevent the development of asthma in children. The pectin found in the apples has been definitively linked to substantial reductions in "LDL" cholesterol, aka "bad" cholesterol. There is also some evidence that lemon assists with the reduction of elevated cholesterol levels as well. The vitamin C in the apples can also help to repair dry skin leaving you with skin that feels healthy and looks youthful.

# Do-mint-ican Republic

Two thirds of a medium sized pineapple
One large stalk of celery
One medium sized cucumber
One cup of mint leaves
One cup of spinach
Half of one lemon, unpeeled

This is a refreshing juice inspired by the beautiful tropical weather and relaxed hospitality of the Dominican Republic. It's minty flavor is sure to delight the taste buds! But this juice isn't just a great tasting, refreshing treat. The heaping amount of pineapple is dense in myriad nutrients your body needs, including vitamins B6 and C, folate, beta carotene, and thiamin. It also contains high levels of minerals like potassium, magnesium, and copper. Studies have shown that regularly consuming pineapple promotes good heart health and can reduce muscle inflammation. For this reason, this juice is great to enjoy after some physical activity.

# Grapefruit Kicker

One large grapefruit (any variety you like)
Three medium sized carrots
One large orange
One thumbnail sized piece of ginger

Grapefruit is great for weight loss and maintaining a healthy
heart. Studies have shown that grapefruit consumption lowers the
risk of diabetes by controlling insulin production and maintaining
consistent blood sugar levels, which also helps to combat obesity.
The high concentration of choline, potassium, lycopene, and
vitamin C in grapefruit all promote heart health and have been
shown to reduce the risk of heart disease.

# Coconut Sundown

Three medium sized carrots
One red apple (Macintosh, Pink Lady, or any other red variety
you like)
Thumbnail sized ginger
One cup of fresh chopped coconut (or substitute for coconut milk)

This is a great tasting juice with a noticeable sweetness that isn't
overpowering. The texture is smooth and creamy, and the "zing"
can be amped up by doubling the ginger content. The color is a
rich and creamy orange and it provides the delicious and
refreshing flavor of coconut while also containing significant
nutrients and anti-oxidants that will energize the body for hours.
A great juice to reinvigorate yourself after a long day at work.

# Just Kale Me Now!

Four leaves of kale
Two large stalks of celery
One small cucumber (or half of one medium sized cucumber)
One medium sized pear, any variety
Half of one lime
One cup of spinach

Kale is such a healthy vegetable that you'll want to consume it as often as possible. You can cycle through the various kale recipes in this book to keep yourself from getting bored. Juices with significant kale quantity and little to no fruit, like this juice, are excellent juices for weight loss. This is because kale is extremely nutrient dense. Drinking kale juice means that you can easily get an entire day's supply of many vitamins and nutrients while hardly consuming any calories.

# Just Beet It!

One beetroot
One medium sized cucumber
Three large stalks of celery
Four large sized carrots
Three leaves of kale
Half a head of romaine lettuce

A delicious would-be green juice with some carrot and beet thrown in. That means that in addition to all of the health benefits of a green juice, you also get the powerful cleansing ability of beet that aids the body in purging toxins and enhancing the health of organs like the kidney and liver.

# Orange Scream

Two large oranges (peeled)
Three large stalks of celery
One medium sized apple
Three medium sized pears
One yam (sweet potato)

Another tasty, creamy juice that is a big summer hit. If it is too sweet, you can add more celery and reduce the number of pears. You could also freeze the juice in popsicle molds and serve it as a refreshing treat to cool down on a hot day.

This juice not only tastes great, it also has some impressive health benefits as well as it is high in folate, niacin, riboflavin, and vitamins B-6 and K. The pears are also high in boron which prevents calcium loss and promotes bone health. The pears also contain high levels of anti-oxidants and can fight high blood pressure as well as reduce inflammation.

# Hawaiian Spice

One large slice of pineapple (chop if needed)
One medium sized apple (any variety you like)
One large cucumber
Half a lemon, peeled
One thumbnail sized piece of ginger
Half a table spoon of pumpkin pie spice

This juice is so sweet you could have it as a dessert while still getting all the healthy benefits of juicing with fruit and vegetables. This juice is consistently a favorite for its great taste, but it can also improve your the function of your cardiovascular system. Studies have shown that consuming the juices from apples and lemons can reduce breathing difficulties, improve oxygen intake, and even prevent the development of asthma in children. The ginger in this juice will also aid in reduction of inflammation which can reduce pain and increase mobility.

# Parsnip Paradise

Two parsnips
Seven medium sized carrots
Three large stalks of celery
One lemon, peeled
One thumb-sized piece of ginger

Parsnips are not commonly juiced, a fact that makes this recipe unique. If you've never tried a parsnip juice, give this one a try. There are lots of great reasons to enjoy parsnip juice as a regular part of your diet. Parsnips contain an exceptionally wide variety of various nutrients, vitamins, and minerals. Parsnips are high in folate, potassium, dietary fiber, and vitamin C.

# Strawberry Lime

Three cups of strawberries
One quarter of a lime, peeled or unpeeled according to taste
Two large apples

Although this is still a healthy juice, it has a relatively high sugar content due to all the fruits. For this reason this juice can be a nice treat once in awhile, but not something you would want to consumer every day. That said, this juice still has some serious health benefits, such as it's detoxifying ability. Strawberries are high in potassium and promote detoxification. They also aid in regulation of the blood pressure.

# The Sour Carrot

Five large carrots
One medium sized Granny Smith apple
One whole lemon, unpeeled
One thumbnail sized piece of ginger root
One clove of garlic

The lemon in this juice gives a strong citrus flavor that is balanced out by the full, earthy carrot flavor that follows. The flavor is too intense for some, and can be toned down by reducing or excluding the ginger and garlic or by adding another apple.

This juice is rich in pectin and as such is a great way to combat high cholesterol. Pectin is found in both apples and carrots and has been definitively linked to substantial reductions in "LDL" cholesterol, aka "bad" cholesterol. There is also some evidence that ginger and lemon assist with the reduction of elevated cholesterol levels as well. The vitamin C in this juice which comes primarily from the carrots can also help to repair dry skin leaving you with skin that feels healthy and looks youthful.

# Breaking Green

Two medium sized green apples
One fennel bulb and stem
Two large cucumbers
One lime, peeled
One half lemon, peeled
Thumb-sized piece of ginger

This is a smooth and flavorful green juice that will delight your tastebuds with a surprising hit of lime and ginger. It is an excellent diuretic juice to use as part of a juice cleanse due to its high water content from the cucumbers. It is also packed full of vitamins, in particular vitamin A and vitamin K, as well as a solid amount of potassium.

# Southern Hospitality

Two large oranges
Three large peaches
Two cups of pineapple
Quarter slice of lemon
One pinch of cayenne pepper (stirred in after juicing)

This tasty juice provides all the vitamin C you need for a whole day. It is also a superb anti-cancer juice. The anti-oxidant power of the vitamin C works to rid the body of free radicals while the limioid compound in the oranges has been shown to fight a variety of different cancers including breast cancer, stomach cancer, colon cancer, and skin cancer.

# Beetastic

Two beetroot
Three medium sized carrots
One stalk of celery
One small cucumber (or half of one medium sized cucumber)

This juice is a great way to make sure you are getting your daily recommended amount of manganese and folate as beetroot is rich in both. This juice is simple and quick to prepare, with no frills, no fruit, and nothing sweet about it. It is a good juice for when you are in a rush or don't have many fruits or vegetables handy, but don't want to skimp on your vegetable consumption.

# Green Stacks

Two cups of spinach
One handful of parsley
Two medium sized Granny Smith apples
Three leaves of kale

It doesn't get much greener than this smooth, eminently drinkable juice. The apples provide a hint of sweetness that will make this drink a favorite even for people who dislike the taste of kale and spinach. The parsley in this juice will also help to reduce the gas and bloating that some people experience when juicing with raw kale. The spinach is a great intestinal tract cleanser that reduces the buildup of waste and facilitates the body's digestive system working efficiently without any digestive issues. The natural laxative found in apples also promotes regular bowel movements. This juice is also rich in vitamins and minerals that the body needs. For example, a small 15 oz glass of this juice provides an entire day's supply of vitamins C and K, as well as the mineral copper.

# The Big Eight

One cup of spinach
One handful of parsley
Four medium sized tomatoes
One small green bell pepper (or half a medium sized green bell pepper)
Two large carrots
Two large stalks of celery
One medium sized cucumber
One small lime
Salt to taste after juicing

This is a slight twist to the classic commercial "V-8" recipe, but it is better because you can produce it yourself fresh in your own kitchen! The juice itself is all about health and weight loss as it is very heavy on the vegetables as opposed to fruit. If you need an energy boost to get you through the day you can't go wrong with this juice as it is rich in both phosphorous and potassium.

This juice is also a great recovery drink after a hard workout. This is due not only to the energy boost the juice delivers, but also due to its ability to reduce inflammation. Spinach is highly alkaline which can help to reduce inflammation. The tomatoes are also rich in inflammation-fighting vitamins and nutrients, many of which are contained in the skin of the tomato.

# Garlic Green

Four chard leaves
Four kale leaves
One cucumber
Two celery stalks
One lime, peeled
Half of one lemon, peeled
Three cloves of garlic (or to taste)

Garlic in the juicer isn't for everyone, but those who like it tend to like it a lot! Garlic is highly nutritious, containing lots of maganese, fiber, selenium, calcium, copper, iron, and vitamins B1, B6, and C. Studies have shown garlic consumption can help prevent and cure the common cold. Garlic also works to lower cholesterol and blood pressure, and may aid with the prevention of certain brain diseases like Alzheimer's disease and dementia. This is probably due at least in part to the high antioxidant concentration.

# Pomegranate Power

One large pomegranate
Two medium sized apples
Two large oranges
One quarter of a lemon
Thumbnail sized piece of ginger root

Pomegranate's truly are a powerhouse when it comes to nutrients and anti-oxidants. Even by the standards of super foods known for their high anti-oxidant concentration, pomegranate leaves most of them in the dust. There is very little fat in a pomegranate and no cholesterol at all. Pomegranate also contains lots of vitamin B5 that helps the body metabolize the macronutrients you consume, which makes this a great juice for anyone trying to lose some weight.

# Berry Pomegranate

One large pomegranate
One cup of raspberries
One cup of blueberries
One quarter of a lemon, peeled

This juice is another tasty anti-oxidant powerhouse like the Pomegranate Power recipe also found in this book. Here the sugar content is increased due to the berries which means this is not such a great weight loss juice. It is however a great source of iron, calcium, zinc, magnesium and phosphorus. The delicious sweet taste of this juice makes it an excellent dessert. You can have a sweet treat while avoiding the many other unhealthy foods typically consumed as dessert.

# Peppermint Strawberry

Two cups of strawberries
Ten leaves of peppermint
Two large apples
Half a lemon

This refreshing juice packs a full day's supply of vitamin C. It also has detoxifying power due to the high potassium content of the strawberries which also helps to regulate blood pressure. In addition to these benefits, strawberries are great for your mental health. Studies have shown that the folic acid found in strawberries facilitates enhanced cognition, memory, and focus. For this reason, this juice would be a perfect choice for studying or working on something that requires prolonged mental focus.

# Can't Beet the Cabbage!

Three large leaves of red cabbage
One beetroot
One large stalk of celery
Three medium carrots
One large orange
One quarter of a pineapple
Three handfuls of spinach
Half a lemon, peeled

The pineapple flavor in this juice helps to even out the earthiness of the beetroot. If it taste too much of beet or cabbage, you can always add some extra pineapple. However you juice it though, this recipe is extremely healthy as it is jam-packed with the vitamins and minerals your body needs.

This juice is a powerful cleanser. The beet juice aids in reducing liver toxicity and combats conditions relating to bile, such as food poisoning, jaundice, hepatitis, diarrhea, and vomiting. The spinach also aids in cleansing the body, especially the intestinal tract, while its high levels of iron help to fortify the blood.

# Green Cleanse

Five large stalks of celery
Two medium sized Granny Smith apples
One medium sized cucumber
Two handfuls of spinach
Five leaves of kale
One quarter of a lemon, peeled
One half of a lime, peeled

They don't come much greener then this tasty, healthy recipe. This juice is a solid choice for anyone wanting to focus on cleansing the body of toxins. Cleansing can be an effective way to jump start a recovery after a binge on unhealthy food or toxic substances like alcohol. It can also be a great way to energize the body even when you normally eat well and live an active lifestyle. If you are doing a juice cleanse, make this drink a staple of the cleanse by drinking it either daily or every other day.

# Melon and More!

Two pears
One apple, any variety
One honeydew melon, chopped
Two handfuls of red grapes

Not only do honeydew melons taste great and yield lots of juice, but they are also a great source of carotenoids. Carotenoids has been shown to promote a variety of desirable health benefits including decreasing the risk of particular cancers and eye diseases. They also have protective benefits for the skin that will help you look and feel younger. Reproductive health and bone density can also improve with regular consumption of carotenoids. The grapes in this juice add a nice, complementary flavor to the melon and more than that, they also contain a variety of anti-inflammatory nutrients that promote longevity!

# Sweet Beet Treat

Two medium sized apples, any variety
Two beetroot
Three large carrots
One third of a medium sized pineapple

There are lots of great reasons to include beets in your diet. First of all, it is rich in key minerals like potassium, magnesium, and iron. It also packs in high levels of vitamins A, B6 and C. In addition, it is rich in anti-oxidants and low in calories. Unfortunately, not everyone enjoys the taste of beetroot due to its distinct "earthy" flavor. If you are one of those people who wants to consume more beets but you just can't stand the taste, this may be the juice that solves your problem! The apple and the pineapple provide enough of a sweet flavor that the taste of beet is toned down greatly. If you find it is two sweet, you can reduce the quantity of pineapple and include some celery or cucumber instead.

# Beet That Cholesterol

One beetroot
One medium sized orange
Five medium sized carrots
Half a lemon
Two large red apples

Moderate, consistent carrot consumption has been shown in studies to reduce cholesterol level by about 10 percent. High cholesterol is a leading cause of heart disease, therefore carrot consumption promotes heart health by reducing your risk of heart disease. Consuming carrots regularly also reduces your risk of a heart attack. Some studies show a dramatic decrease in heart attack risk when carrot consumption is maintained over the course of a year. Drinking this juice daily will lower your risk of a heart attack.

# Green relief

Two medium sized green bell peppers
Three stalks of celery
Two cups of spinach
Two medium sized green apples
Three medium sized carrots
Twenty-five grapes, any variety you like
One medium sized tomato

This is a great juice for boosting your immune system, lowering
your blood pressure, and losing weight. The high levels of
potassium and magnesium in this juice, as well as the two cups of
spinach, work together to lower elevated blood pressure. The
juice from the green bell pepper contains powerful antioxidants
that contribute to a reduction in cholesterol.

# Morning Kale

Three large stalks of celery
Half an English cucumber
Six leaves of kale
One medium sized apples
Two cups of spinach
Half a lemon

This juice is great for weight loss while still quenching your thirst with a delicious taste. It contains a significant amount of raw kale. Kale is considered a "super food" and is ideal for weight loss due to its high concentration of nutrients and low calorie content. It is among the most nutrient-dense vegetables available and this juice makes sure you can easily consume this amazing vegetable daily. Kale is also a significant source of organo-sulfur compounds. Studies show these compounds are effective at fighting many different types of cancer. One of the many amazing qualities of kale is that it can actually contribute to a destruction of cancer cells within the body.

In addition to fighting cancer that already exists in the body, kale has also been shown to prevent cancer from occurring in the first place. The sulforaphane contents of kale has been shown to reduce the risk of cancer from occurring in the body.

This drink also contains spinach, which is another vegetable studies have shown to be effective in fighting and preventing various types of cancer. The powerful anti-oxidants contained in this vegetable contribute to the deceleration of cancerous cell production and division.

# Zesty Cabbage

One quarter of a small head of red cabbage
One medium sized red apple (Gala, Macintosh, etc.)
Three cloves of garlic
One thumb-sized piece of ginger root
One cup of spinach
Four medium sized carrots
Half a lemon
Half a lime

This is a great juice if you're looking to sooth any digestive issues you may be experiencing. The carrots work to cleanse the liver while stimulating a release of bile that is a key component of proper digestions. Juicing with lemon and ginger root not only adds a kick to the juice's flavor, but they also both aid in digestion by reducing gas buildup. Finally, the spinach works to cleanse the intestinal tract while promoting proper digestion.

# Minty Citrus

Two large oranges
One medium sized apple, any variety
One cucumber
One lemon, peeled
Two cups of mint leaves

This is a great pre-workout beverage as it has just enough sugar in the oranges to get you energized, but not so much that you'll endure a sudden post-sugar crash. The generous helping of mint adds a unique kick to the flavor of this juice that compliments the other fruits and vegetables very well. Mint also delivers some surprising health benefits. Mint has antimicrobial properties and has also been shown to sooth a queasy stomach.

# Strawberry Lemon Lime

Four medium sized carrots
One medium sized cucumber
One and a half cups of strawberries
One medium sized apple
One half of a lemon, peeled
One lime, peeled

This is a filling juice that provides a delicious way to get all the benefits of carrots while masking their flavor with the sweet taste of strawberries. The combination of carrots and strawberries is a favorite flavor of many people who juice regularly. In terms of health benefits, this juice provides a powerful boost to the immune system. The carrots boost the production and efficiency of the white blood cells, which help to defend the body against a variety of infections. The high vitamin C content of the strawberries aid the body in fighting and preventing colds and the flu.

# Peachers Daughter

Five large peaches
Two medium sized carrots
One medium sized apples
One medium sized orange
Half a lemon, peeled

This recipe yields a smooth, sweet, peachy drink. Even if you dislike the taste of carrots, it is important to consume them regularly and in this juice you can barely taste them. Regular carrot consumption has been shown to reduce "bad" LDL cholesterol levels by about 10 percent. High cholesterol is a leading cause of heart disease, therefore carrot consumption promotes heart health by reducing your risk of heart disease and also reducing your risk of a heart attack. This juice can radically improve your heart health while still tasting like a dream. The peaches are a bit high in sugar though so this is not a great daily juice for someone trying to lose weight.

# Apple of my Eye

Four medium sized apples
One English cucumber
Two stalks of celery
One large orange, peeled
One thumbnail sized piece of ginger root

A tasty apple juice with a ginger kick! The celery, although perhaps not the tastiest produce, is high in vitamins and minerals that help to maintain the skin's youthful elasticity and aid complexion. Celery can also help to calm the nerves and reduce high blood pressure. The orange juice also helps to protect the skin by attacking and eliminating free radicals within the body.

# Parsley delight

Three cups of parsley
One medium sized apple (any variety)
One medium sized cucumber
One cup of spinach
One half of a lime, peeled

This juice is great for cleansing the body of toxins and facilitating enhanced liver and kidney function. The significant quantity of parsley also makes this juice a powerful immune system booster. Parsley has been shown to promote a strong immune system that keeps the whole body healthy and wards of colds, the flu, and other common ailments. Parsley is nutrient dense and provides a significant source of numerous vitamins including vitamin A, vitamin B 12, vitamin C, and vitamin K.

# Sweet and Sour Celery

Four stalks of celery
One peeled lemon
One peeled lime
Two medium sized Granny Smith apples (granny smith)
One medium sized pear, any variety you like
Four cups of spinach
Four leaves of kale


The sour lemon and sweet apple create an interesting flavor combination. Even if you are not a fan of the taste of kale, you will probably still like this juice as the taste is masked by the other ingredients. This is a great juice for improving your complexion and making you feel and look vibrant and youthful. The juice from the lemon functions as a natural antiseptic that promotes skin health. The sodium in the celery is jam-packed with minerals and vitamins which promote elasticity and youthful tightness in the skin. Between the apples and the kale, you're also consuming significant quantities of vitamins A, C, E, and K, all of which prevent the appearance of premature aging by reducing free radicals in the body.

# Mango Unchained

Two large mango, peeled (or three to four smaller sized mangos)
Half a lemon, peeled
One medium sized apple
One medium sized clementine

This juice adds a little twist to the fresh mango flavor everyone loves! It also gives you a substantial dose of vitamins A, B, C, E, K, folate, niacin, riboflavin, calcium, and iron.

# Melon Horizon

One quarter of a watermelon, rind removed
One quarter of a pineapple, rind removed
Four strawberries
One cup of blueberries
Half a cup of raspberries
Half a lime, peeled

This juice is consistently a favorite for it's sweet, delicious taste. Unfortunately this sweet taste comes with a relatively high amount of sugar, meaning this juice really is more of a "treat" than something you would want to enjoy daily. Despite the sugar, the juice still has many health benefits, such as being rich in antioxidants due to the strawberries and blueberries. This juice is a great way to treat yourself without feeling too guilty.

# Pineapple Punch

Half a medium sized pineapple
Two large carrots
Half of one lemon, peeled
Mix with an equal part of club soda after juicing

This is a great tasting, healthy punch to enjoy at a party or with friends. The carrots in this juice promote a healthy cleanse by functioning as a diuretic and forcing excess fluid out of the body. In addition, the pineapple is rich in vitamins B6 and C, folate, beta carotene, and thiamin. This juice is a great way to ensure you get the recommended daily dose of potassium, magnesium, and copper. The pineapples and carrots also promote good heart health and can reduce the risk of heart disease.

# Once you go Blackberry

One cup of blackberries
One English cucumber
Three kiwi
One medium sized pear
Five leaves of peppermint

A smooth juice with just a hint of sour, this juice is always a hit with those who love the taste of blackberries. Pear juice contains high levels of antioxidants, as does the kiwi juice due to it's high levels of copper, iron, and vitamins C and E. The anti-oxidant power of this juice provides a boost to your immune system that can help the body to prevent or quickly fight off colds or the flu.

# Sam I Yam

One yam (sweet potato)
Sixt large carrots
Two beetroot


This juice is full of root vegetables that deliver a robust cleanse with a creamy, earthy flavor. Beet juice greatly reduces toxicity of the liver and improves conditions like hepatitis, food poisoning, diarrhea, vomiting, and jaundice. It is a great "reset" for your body after consuming alcohol as it cleanses the liver of the toxic alcohol it has been working to remove from your body. In addition to the cleansing power of beets, the carrots in this juice aid in the cleanse by functioning as a diuretic and forcing excess fluid out of the body.

Beets don't just cleanse the liver though, they also help to cleanse the blood, colon, and gall bladder. Within the bloodstream, the high iron content works to rebuild your red blood cell count so that your body can benefit from increased access to oxygen. In addition, the liver aids in the metabolization of fat. Keeping your liver cleansed and running efficiently promotes weight loss efficiency.

# Turmeric Orange Juice

Three thumbnail sized piece of turmeric
Two large oranges
Two clementines
One thumbnail sized piece of ginger

Studies have widely recognized curcumin, a component of turmeric, as a powerful anti-inflammatory agent. In fact, turmeric contains at least five other components that also have anti-inflammatory effects. Further, more recent studies indicate strong evidence that turmeric also has anti-cancer properties. Despite this, our typical diets don't contain nearly enough turmeric! Juicing with turmeric is a convenient and delicious way to make sure you avail yourself of its many health benefits.

# Coconut Surprise

One medium sized coconut (scoop the meat out and discard the shell)
One large cucumber
One medium sized orange
One medium sized peaches

This tasty tropical juice boasts big quantities of copper, iron, potassium, phosphorus, magnesium, zinc, and selenium. These minerals are important for a variety of important functions within the body. Copper and iron work together to improve the flow of oxygen through the bloodstream by boosting the production of red and white blood cells. Selenium contributes to the proper function of the immune system as well as the reproductive system. Magnesium promotes a healthy bone density and together with zinc helps the body to process the macronutrients we consume and turn them into energy the body can use.

# Guava and Green

Two medium sized guava, or one large guava (peeled or unpeeled according to preference)
One medium sized Granny Smith apple
One large cucumber
Two stalks of celery
One kiwi

Guava is not a popular fruit in many Western countries, which is really unfortunate for us! Guava is a delicious "super fruit" widely consumed in some tropical countries. It earned its reputation as a super fruit due to its high concentration of a wide variety of nutrients and its many health benefits. Among other vitamins, minerals, and nutrients, Guava is particularly rich in copper, vitamin C, lycopene, and antioxidants. If you aren't able to find guava at your local chain grocery store then try a smaller produce market, especially one that carries a variety of ethnic foods.

# Circulatory Boost Juice

Two large carrots
One handful of parsley
Three medium sized Granny Smith apples
One stalks of celery
Five stalks of asparagus
One medium sized cucumber


This recipe yields a mild tasting juice with a kick to boost your blood circulation. Studies have shown that a lack of histamines in the body can contribute to poor circulation. The juiced asparagus stalks are a great source of folic acid which promotes the production of histamines and parsley has also been shown to improve blood flow within the body.

# Detox in a Glass

Two beetroots
Three cups of spinach
Three large stalks of celery
One medium sized cucmber

This juice is a great choice after a weekend of indulging in alcohol. The beets in this juice works to reduce alcohol toxicity in the liver and promotes recovery by cleansing the blood and aiding in the delivering of oxygen via the bloodstream. The spinach also has cleansing properties and aids the restoration of the body's circulatory system. It has also been shown to promote brain health, which can help you recover from the mental fog a hang over faster. Finally, the calcium and magnesium in the celery stalks have been shown to ease agitation of the central nervous system.

# Natura-lax

One beetroot
Three medium sized apple
Four medium sized carrots
Two cups of spinach
Two large celery stalks
One cup of raspberries

This juice has a heavy, earthy flavor from the carrots and beets.
Like the other beetroot juices in this book, this one is another
great internal cleanser. The beet juice reduces toxicity in the liver
which can deliver fast relief from accidental food poisoning,
diarrhea, and vomiting. It is also an excellent cure for a hangover
due to the liver cleansing beetroot in the juice. In addition to the
beetroot, the apples you use in this juice contain a natural
laxative. Apple juice facilitates regular bowel movements which
add to the cleansing power of this juice.

# Sweet Potato Paradise

One medium sized yam (sweet potato)
One beetroot
Two large carrot
Two medium sized apples
One medium sized clementine, peeled

This juice will make you feel vibrant and energized as it delivers a great source of fast energy. Your body can quickly digest the carbohydrates in the beetroot and use them to fuel your body throughout the day.

This juice also facilitates proper digestion within the body and can aid indigestion. This is due to the natural laxative properties of apples. The juice in the apple promotes regular bowel movements. Carrots and beets also promote regular bowel movements by cleansing the liver and stimulating additional bile release which can aid constipation.

# Energetic Cleanse

One beetroot
Two large sized Granny Smith apples
Four medium sized carrots
Thumb sized piece of ginger
Two large stalks of celery
One lemon, peeled

A champion cleanser! The root vegetables in this juice detoxify the liver, strengthen the blood, and aid with the reduction of any condition related to toxicity in the body, such as hepatitis, food poisoning, jaundice, and a hang over. While cleansing the body, this juice also provides an immediate energy boost that can last for hours.

# I Cantaloupe, I'm Married!

Half a medium sized cantaloupe
One peeled mango
One medium sized pear, any variety

This is a great tasting juice that is best enjoyed in moderation due to the sugar content and the relative lack of health benefits compared to most of the other juices in this book. Despite its status as more of a "dessert juice" it still manages to contain high levels of potassium as well as vitamins A and C. This can make it a good choice for warding off a cold or flu, as well as maintaining or improving the health of your skin, eyes, and immune system.

# Papaya by the beach

Two papaya
Three peaches
One clove of garlic
One thumb sized piece of ginger

This juice is a good source of vitamins A and C. It also contains
plenty of antioxidants and potassium. If you want more of a kick,
double the garlic and ginger content!

# Immuni-Juice

Six thumb sized pieces or turmeric
Three medium sized pears
Two medium sized carrots
Two medium sized apples
Five large celery stalks
One thumbnail sized piece of ginger
One lemon, peeled

This juice works to boost your immune system and can provide quick relief for cold or flu symptoms. If you are suffering from a fever in particular, consider doubling the quantity of ginger you are juicing. The heavy lemon content in this juice facilitates perspiration while reducing feelings of nausea or dizziness. This juice also contains many pears which are great for preventing a cold or flu or fighting one off by fortifying the body's immune system.

# Sour Ginger

Four thumb sized pieces of ginger
One medium sized cucumber
Two medium sized apple, any variety
Two lemons, peeled
One clove of garlic

Ginger isn't a flavor for everyone, but those who like it will definitely want to give this juice a try. Even those who do not like the taste of ginger may still appreciate this juice for it's effect on the digestive system. Ginger and lemon have both been shown to ease digestive issues such as nausea, dizziness, motion sickness, vomiting, or an upset stomach, and this juice has both ingredients in abundance! In fact, studies have shown that ginger is actually superior to popular prescription medication when it comes to providing relief for digestive problems!

# Rabbit Vision

Eight medium sized carrots
One large cucumber
One thumb sized piece of ginger root
Half a lemon
Half a lime

This carrot heavy juice is a great way to improve your eyesight and prevent certain diseases that effect the eye. Studies have shown that a deficiency in vitamin A can impair the ability to see in dim light. This juice contains over 300% of the required daily dose of vitamin A which makes it ideal for boosting this crucial vitamin in those who may be deficient. The beta-carotene in this juice is also an effective way to prevent macular degeneration, a common condition that impairs sight as the body ages. Studies have shown that people who consistently consume large quantities of beta-carotene can cut their risk of macular degeneration in half.

# Kale And Pepper Juice

Six leaves of kale
One cup of collard greens
One medium sized green bell pepper
Three medium sized pears
Two handfuls of cilantro
Three medium sized carrots

In addition to promoting overall bodily health, this juice can be an effective cancer deterrent. The collard greens are rich in nutrients that have powerful cancer fighting properties. Studies have shown both kale and collard greens can be beneficial at fighting and preventing breast cancer, prostate cancer, colon cancer, and other cancers.

This juice is also a great juice for weight loss. The kale leaves and collard greens are extremely nutrient-dense, meaning they add very few calories to this juice while still managing to deliver a significant quantity of nutrients and anti-oxidants.

# Broccoli Apple Juice

One cup of broccoli florets
Five medium sized apples
Half a lemon, peeled
Half a lime, peeled

Most of us don't eat enough broccoli, which is unfortunate because this vegetable contains high levels of vitamins B, C, and K, as well as several important minerals. Broccoli is "nutrient dense" meaning that it is very low in calories while still being high in a variety of nutrients. Juicing with broccoli has been shown to help prevent the deterioration of eye sight due to age-related conditions like macular degeneration.

Broccoli is also a powerful cleanser and detoxifier. Some of the nutrients contained in broccoli (such as glucoraphanin, gluconasturtiin, and glucobrassicin) facilitate a natural detoxification process in the body by working to activate, neutralize, and eliminate a variety of harmful contaminants.

# Minty Garlic

One large pink grapefruit
Three clementine
Half a cup of mint
Four cloves of garlic
One thumb sized piece of ginger

This is a delicious juices that packs a high dose of vitamin C and antioxidants to energize and strengthen the immune system. This juice is also surprisingly filling due to the grapefruit content, which makes it a great choice for a juice fast or weight loss regimen.

# Young Apple

Four Granny Smith apples
One clementine, peeled
One medium cucumber
One cup of spinach
One lime, peeled
One lemon, peeled

Studies have shown that consuming the juices from apples and lemons can reduce breathing difficulties, improve oxygen intake, and even prevent the development of asthma in children. The pectin found in the apples has been definitively linked to substantial reductions in "LDL" cholesterol, aka "bad" cholesterol. There is also some evidence that lemon assists with the reduction of elevated cholesterol levels as well. The vitamin C in the apples can also help to repair dry skin leaving you with skin that feels healthy and looks youthful.

# Sea Breeze

Half a medium sized pineapple
Two large stalks of celery
One cup of spinach
Half of one lime, unpeeled

The pineapple in this delicious juice contains many nutrients your body needs, including vitamins B6 and C, folate, beta carotene, and thiamin. It also contains high levels of minerals like potassium, magnesium, and copper. Studies have shown that regularly consuming pineapple promotes good heart health and can reduce muscle inflammation. For this reason, this juice is great to enjoy after some physical activity.

# Grapefruit Fat Burner

One large ruby red grapefruit
Two medium sized carrots
Two medium sized oranges
One thumb sized piece of ginger

Grapefruit is great for weight loss and maintaining a healthy
heart. Studies have shown that grapefruit consumption lowers the
risk of diabetes by controlling insulin production and maintaining
consistent blood sugar levels, which also helps to combat obesity.
The high concentration of choline, potassium, lycopene, and
vitamin C in grapefruit all promote heart health and have been
shown to reduce the risk of heart disease.

# Coconut Carrot Juice

One cup of fresh chopped coconut (or substitute for coconut milk)
Three medium sized carrots
Two medium sized apples
One English cucumber
One thumb sized ginger

This is a great tasting juice with a noticeable sweetness that isn't overpowering. The texture is smooth and creamy, and the "zing" can be amped up by doubling the ginger content. The color is a rich and creamy orange and it provides the delicious and refreshing flavor of coconut while also containing significant nutrients and anti-oxidants that will energize the body for hours. A great juice to reinvigorate yourself after a long day at work.

# Kale-ry Juice

Six leaves of kale
Five large stalks of celery
One medium sized pear, any variety
Half of one lime
One cup of spinach

Kale is such a healthy vegetable that you'll want to consume it as often as possible. Juices with significant kale quantity and little to no fruit, like this juice, are excellent juices for weight loss. This is because kale is extremely nutrient dense. Drinking kale juice means that you can easily get an entire day's supply of many vitamins and nutrients while hardly consuming any calories.

# Earthy Greens

One beetroot
One medium sized cucumber
Four large sized carrots
Three leaves of kale
Two medium sized apples

A delicious mix between a green juice and a hearty, earthy juice.
That means that in addition to all of the health benefits of a green
juice, you also get the powerful cleansing ability of beet that aids
the body in purging toxins and enhancing the health of organs like
the kidney and liver.

# Earthy Orange

Two large oranges (peeled)
Four large stalks of celery
One medium sized apple
Two medium sized pears
One yam (sweet potato)

This is a tasty, creamy juice that is just a little bit sweet. This juice not only tastes great, it also has some impressive health benefits as well as it is high in folate, niacin, riboflavin, and vitamins B-6 and K. The pears are also high in boron which prevents calcium loss and promotes bone health. The pears also contain high levels of anti-oxidants and can fight high blood pressure as well as reduce inflammation.

# Hoola Juice

Half a medium sized pineapple (chop if needed)
One medium sized apple (any variety you like)
Half a lemon, peeled
One thumb sized piece of ginger
Half a table spoon of pumpkin pie spice, added after juicing

This juice is so sweet you could have it as a dessert while still getting all the healthy benefits of juicing with fruit and vegetables. This juice is consistently a favorite for its great taste, but it can also improve your the function of your cardiovascular system. Studies have shown that consuming the juices from apples and lemons can reduce breathing difficulties, improve oxygen intake, and even prevent the development of asthma in children. The ginger in this juice will also aid in reduction of inflammation which can reduce pain and increase mobility.

# Parsnippity Zinger

Two parsnips
Five medium sized carrots
Two large stalks of celery
One medium sized cucumber
One lemon, peeled
One thumb sized piece of ginger

A tasty parsnip juice that is uncommon, but a great way to add variety to the diet of a veteran juicer. There are lots of great reasons to enjoy parsnip juice as a regular part of your diet. Parsnips contain an exceptionally wide variety of various nutrients, vitamins, and minerals. Parsnips are high in folate, potassium, dietary fiber, and vitamin C.

# Sour Strawberry Sunset

Three cups of strawberries
Three large apples
One lime, peeled
One lemon, peeled


Although this is still a healthy juice, it has a relatively high sugar content due to all the fruits. For this reason this juice can be a nice treat once in awhile, but not something you would want to consumer every day. That said, this juice still has some serious health benefits, such as it's detoxifying ability. Strawberries are high in potassium and promote detoxification. They also aid in regulation of the blood pressure.

# Carrot Top

Five large carrots
One handful of parsley
One medium sized cucumber
One medium sized Granny Smith apple
Half a lemon, unpeeled
One thumb sized piece of ginger root
One clove of garlic

The lemon in this juice gives a strong citrus flavor that is balanced out by the full, earthy carrot flavor that follows. The flavor is too intense for some, and can be toned down by reducing or excluding the ginger and garlic or by adding another apple.

This juice is rich in pectin and as such is a great way to combat high cholesterol. Pectin is found in both apples and carrots and has been definitively linked to substantial reductions in "LDL" cholesterol, aka "bad" cholesterol. There is also some evidence that ginger and lemon assist with the reduction of elevated cholesterol levels as well. The vitamin C in this juice which comes primarily from the carrots can also help to repair dry skin leaving you with skin that feels healthy and looks youthful.

# Green Surprise

Three medium sized green apples
One fennel bulb and stem
One medium sized cucumbers
One lime, peeled
One half lemon, peeled
One thumb sized piece of ginger

This is a smooth and flavorful green juice that will delight your tastebuds with a surprising hit of fennel, lime and ginger. It is an excellent diuretic juice to use as part of a juice cleanse due to its high water content from the cucumbers. It is also packed full of vitamins, in particular vitamin A and vitamin K, as well as a solid amount of potassium.

# The Georgia Way

Four large peaches
Two small oranges (or one medium sized orange)
Two cups of pineapple, chopped
Half a lemon, peeled
One pinch of cayenne pepper (stirred in after juicing)

This tasty juice provides all the vitamin C you need for a whole day. It is also a superb anti-cancer juice. The anti-oxidant power of the vitamin C works to rid the body of free radicals while the limioid compound in the oranges has been shown to fight a variety of different cancers including breast cancer, stomach cancer, colon cancer, and skin cancer.

# Quick Beet Down

Two beetroot
Four medium sized carrots
One stalk of celery
One English cucumber
One clove of garlic

This juice is a great way to make sure you are getting your daily recommended amount of manganese and folate as beetroot is rich in both. This juice is simple and quick to prepare, with no frills, no fruit, and nothing sweet about it. It is a good juice for when you are in a rush or don't have many fruits or vegetables handy, but don't want to skimp on your vegetable consumption.

# Jolly Green Juice

Three cups of spinach
One handful of parsley
Two medium sized Granny Smith apples
Three leaves of kale
One English Cucumber

The apples provide a hint of sweetness that will make this drink a favorite even for people who dislike the taste of kale and spinach. The parsley in this juice will also help to reduce the gas and bloating that some people experience when juicing with raw kale. The spinach is a great intestinal tract cleanser that reduces the buildup of waste and facilitates the body's digestive system working efficiently without any digestive issues. The natural laxative found in apples also promotes regular bowel movements. This juice is also rich in vitamins and minerals that the body needs. For example, a small 15 oz glass of this juice provides an entire day's supply of vitamins C and K, as well as the mineral copper.

# The Full Stack

One cup of spinach
One handful of parsley
One medium sized tomatoes
One medium sized red bell pepper
Three large carrots
Three large stalks of celery
One medium sized cucumber
One lime, peeled
One lemon, peeled

This juice is all about health and weight loss as it is very heavy on the vegetables as opposed to fruit. If you need an energy boost to get you through the day you can't go wrong with this juice as it is rich in both phosphorous and potassium.

This juice is also a great recovery drink after a hard workout. This is due not only to the energy boost the juice delivers, but also due to its ability to reduce inflammation. Spinach is highly alkaline which can help to reduce inflammation. The tomatoes are also rich in inflammation-fighting vitamins and nutrients, many of which are contained in the skin of the tomato.

# Memory Juice

One cucumber
Four chard leaves
Six kale leaves
Three celery stalks
One lime, peeled
Half of one lemon, peeled
Four cloves of garlic

Garlic in the juicer isn't for everyone, but those who like it tend to like it a lot! Garlic is highly nutritious, containing lots of maganese, fiber, selenium, calcium, copper, iron, and vitamins B1, B6, and C. Studies have shown garlic consumption can help prevent and cure the common cold. Garlic also works to lower cholesterol and blood pressure, and may aid with the prevention of certain brain diseases like Alzheimer's disease and dementia. This is probably due at least in part to the high antioxidant concentration.

# Peace and Pomegranate

One large pomegranate
Three medium sized red apples (any red variety)
One large oranges
Two clementines
One half of a lemon
Thumb sized piece of ginger root

Pomegranate is a great source of nutrients and anti-oxidants. Even by the standards of super foods known for their high anti-oxidant concentration, pomegranate leaves most of them in the dust.
There is very little fat in a pomegranate and no cholesterol at all. Pomegranate also contains lots of vitamin B5 that helps the body metabolize the macronutrients you consume, which makes this a great juice for anyone trying to lose some weight.

# Sour Berry Pome-tastic

One large pomegranate
Half a cup of raspberries
Half a cup of blueberries
One medium sized cucumber
One lemon, peeled
Half a small lime, peeled

This juice is a tasty anti-oxidant powerhouse and a great source of iron, calcium, zinc, magnesium and phosphorus.

# Strawberry Wonderful

Three cups of strawberries
One medium sized apple, any variety
One medium sized pear, any variety
Half a lemon, peeled

This refreshing juice packs a full day's supply of vitamin C. It also has detoxifying power due to the high potassium content of the strawberries which also helps to regulate blood pressure. In addition to these benefits, strawberries are great for your mental health. Studies have shown that the folic acid found in strawberries facilitates enhanced cognition, memory, and focus. For this reason, this juice would be a perfect choice for studying or working on something that requires prolonged mental focus.

# Sweet Mother Earth

Three large stalks of celery
Two large leaves of red cabbage
One beetroot
Two medium carrots
One large orange
One quarter of a pineapple
Three handfuls of spinach

The pineapple flavor in this juice helps to even out the earthiness of the beetroot. If it taste too much of beet or cabbage, you can always add some extra pineapple. However you juice it though, this recipe is extremely healthy as it is packed with the vitamins and minerals your body needs.

This juice is a powerful cleanser. The beet juice aids in reducing liver toxicity and combats conditions relating to bile, such as food poisoning, jaundice, hepatitis, diarrhea, and vomiting. The spinach also aids in cleansing the body, especially the intestinal tract, while its high levels of iron help to fortify the blood.

# Green Rolling Hills

Six large stalks of celery
Three medium sized Granny Smith apples
Two handfuls of spinach
Five leaves of kale
One lime, peeled

This juice is a solid choice for anyone wanting to focus on weight loss and cleansing the body of toxins. Cleansing can be an effective way to jump start a recovery after a binge on unhealthy food or toxic substances like alcohol. It can also be a great way to energize the body even when you normally eat well and live an active lifestyle. If you are doing a juice cleanse, make this drink a staple of the cleanse by drinking it either daily or every other day.

# Mighty Melon Grape Juice

Two medium sized apples, any variety
Two medium sized pears, any variety
Half a honeydew melon, chopped
One handful of green grapes

Not only do honeydew melons taste great and yield lots of juice, but they are also a great source of carotenoids. Carotenoids has been shown to promote a variety of desirable health benefits including decreasing the risk of particular cancers and eye diseases. They also have protective benefits for the skin that will help you look and feel younger. Reproductive health and bone density can also improve with regular consumption of carotenoids. The grapes in this juice add a nice, complementary flavor to the melon and more than that, they also contain a variety of anti-inflammatory nutrients that promote longevity!

# Give me the Beets!

Two beetroot
Three medium sized Granny Smith apples
Two large carrots
One third of a medium sized pineapple

Beetroot is rich in key minerals like potassium, magnesium, and iron. It also packs in high levels of vitamins A, B6 and C. In addition, it is rich in anti-oxidants and low in calories.

# Sweet Antioxidant Juice

One kiwi
Two cups of blackberries
One quarter pineapple
One medium sized pear
One thumb sized piece of ginger
Half a lemon, peeled

A smooth juice with just a hint of sour, this juice is always a hit
with those who love the taste of blackberries. Pear juice contains
high levels of antioxidants, as does the kiwi juice due to it's high
levels of copper, iron, and vitamins C and E. The antioxidant
power of this juice provides a boost to your immune system that
can help the body to prevent or quickly fight off colds or the flu.

# Mister Root Juice

Six medium sized carrots
One beetroot
One yam (sweet potato)
Two Granny Smith apples

This juice is full of root vegetables that deliver a robust cleanse and reduces toxicity of the liver and improves conditions like hepatitis, food poisoning, diarrhea, vomiting, and jaundice. It is a great "reset" for your body after consuming alcohol as it cleanses the liver of the toxic alcohol it has been working to remove from your body. In addition to the cleansing power of beets, the carrots in this juice aid in the cleanse by functioning as a diuretic and forcing excess fluid out of the body.

Beets don't just cleanse the liver though, they also help to cleanse the blood, colon, and gall bladder. Within the bloodstream, the high iron content works to rebuild your red blood cell count so that your body can benefit from increased access to oxygen. In addition, the liver aids in the metabolization of fat. Keeping your liver cleansed and running efficiently promotes weight loss efficiency.

# Inflammation Remedy

One large orange
Three medium sized carrots
Two large stalks of celery
One thumbnail sized piece of turmeric
One thumbnail sized piece of ginger
Half of one lemon, unpeeled
Five leaves of peppermint

Studies have widely recognized curcumin, a component of turmeric, as a powerful anti-inflammatory agent. In fact, turmeric contains at least five other components that also have anti-inflammatory effects. Further, more recent studies indicate strong evidence that turmeric also has anti-cancer properties. Despite this, our typical diets don't contain nearly enough turmeric! Juicing with turmeric is a convenient and delicious way to make sure you avail yourself of its many health benefits.

# Impeached

Five medium sized peaches
One quarter of a medium sized coconut (scoop the meat out and
discard the shell)
One large orange

This tasty tropical juice boasts big quantities of copper, iron,
potassium, phosphorus, magnesium, zinc, and selenium. These
minerals are important for a variety of important functions within
the body. Copper and iron work together to improve the flow of
oxygen through the bloodstream by boosting the production of
red and white blood cells. Selenium contributes to the proper
function of the immune system as well as the reproductive
system. Magnesium promotes a healthy bone density and together
with zinc helps the body to process the macronutrients we
consume and turn them into energy the body can use.

# Sun Kissed Guava

Two medium sized guava, or one large guava (peeled or unpeeled according to preference)
One large orange, peeled
One medium sized apple, any variety
Half a lemon, peeled

Guava is not a popular fruit in many Western countries, which is really unfortunate for us! Guava is a delicious "super fruit" widely consumed in some tropical countries. It earned its reputation as a super fruit due to its high concentration of a wide variety of nutrients and its many health benefits. Among other vitamins, minerals, and nutrients, Guava is particularly rich in copper, vitamin C, lycopene, and antioxidants. If you aren't able to find guava at your local chain grocery store then try a smaller produce market, especially one that carries a variety of ethnic foods.

# Pump It Up!

Three large carrots
One handful of parsley
Four stalks of celery
Two stalks of asparagus
One medium sized stalk of broccoli
One medium sized cucumber
Two table spoons of extra virgin olive oil (stir in after juicing)

This juice is an easy way to load up on folic acid and histamines which promote blood flow, improved circulation, and can even boost the libido! Parsley has also been shown to improve blood flow which can enhance sexual stimulation.

# I Heart This Juice

One beetroot
Two medium sized apples
Three medium sized carrots
Half a lemon, peeled
Half a lime, unpeeled
Two large peeled oranges

Moderate, consistent carrot consumption has been shown in studies to reduce cholesterol level by about 10 percent. High cholesterol is a leading cause of heart disease, therefore carrot consumption promotes heart health by reducing your risk of heart disease. Consuming carrots regularly also reduces your risk of a heart attack. In fact, some studies show a dramatic decrease in heart attack risk when carrot consumption is maintained over the course of a year. Drinking this juice daily will could lower your risk of a heart attack by up to two thirds!

# The Red Green Show

Three Roma Tomatoes
One medium sized green bell pepper
Two cups of spinach
Two medium sized green apples
Three medium sized carrots
Fifteen green grapes
Two large celery stalks

This is a great juice for boosting your immune system, lowering your blood pressure, and losing weight. The high levels of potassium and magnesium in this juice, as well as the two cups of spinach, work together to lower elevated blood pressure. The juice from the green bell pepper contains powerful antioxidants that contribute to a reduction in cholesterol.

# Fresh Garden Kale

Six leaves of kale
Half a medium sized cucumber
Three medium sized apples
One medium sized bartlett pear
Two cups of spinach
One lemon

A delicious, Kale based juice that is excellent for weight loss! Kale is considered a "super food" and is ideal for weight loss due to its high concentration of nutrients and low calorie content. It is among the most nutrient-dense vegetables available and this juice makes sure you can easily consume this amazing vegetable daily. Kale is also a significant source of organo-sulfur compounds. Studies show these compounds are effective at fighting many different types of cancer. One of the many amazing qualities of kale is that it can actually contribute to a destruction of cancer cells within the body.

In addition to fighting cancer that already exists in the body, kale has also been shown to prevent cancer from occurring in the first place. The sulforaphane contents of kale has been shown to reduce the risk of cancer from occurring in the body.

In addition to the cancer fighting and preventing power of kale, this drink also contains spinach, which is another vegetable studies have shown to be effective in fighting and preventing various types of cancer. The powerful anti-oxidants contained in this vegetable contribute to the deceleration of cancerous cell production and division.

# Cabbage Apple Aid

One quarter of a small head of green cabbage
Two medium sized Granny Smith apples
One cup of spinach
One thumb sized piece of ginger root
Four medium sized carrots
One lemon, peeled

This juice helps sooth any digestive issues you may be experiencing. The natural laxative in apples can aid with constipation and promote regular bowel movements. The carrots work to cleanse the liver while stimulating a release of bile that is a key component of proper digestions. Juicing with lemon and ginger root not only adds a kick to the juice's flavor, but they also both aid in digestion by reducing gas buildup. Finally, the spinach works to cleanse the intestinal tract while promoting proper digestion.

# Minty Fresh and Ready

Four clementines, peeled
Two apples, any variety
Three large celery stalks
One lemon, peeled
Two cups of mint leaves

This is a great pre-workout beverage as it has just enough sugar in the oranges to get you energized, but not so much that you'll endure a sudden post-sugar crash. The generous helping of mint adds a unique kick to the flavor of this juice that compliments the other fruits and vegetables very well. Mint also delivers some surprising health benefits. Mint has antimicrobial properties and has also been shown to sooth a queasy stomach.

# Sweet and Sour Berry Surprise

Four medium sized carrots
One cup of strawberries
Half a cup of blueberries
One medium sized apple
One half of a lemon, peeled
Five cloves of garlic

This juice provides a powerful boost to the immune system. The carrots boost the production and efficiency of the white blood cells, which help to defend the body against a variety of infections. The high vitamin C content of the strawberries aid the body in fighting and preventing colds and the flu.

# Peachy Peppermint

Eight medium sized carrots (or six large carrots)
Three medium sized apples
One medium sized orange
Three large peaches
Half a lemon, peeled
Five leaves of peppermint

Don't be fooled by all the carrots you're juicing, the end result of this recipe is a smooth, sweet, peachy drink perfect for relaxing outside on a nice summer day. Even if you dislike the taste of carrots, it is important to consume them regularly. Regular carrot consumption has been shown to reduce "bad" LDL cholesterol levels by about 10 percent. High cholesterol is a leading cause of heart disease, therefore carrot consumption promotes heart health by reducing your risk of heart disease and also reducing your risk of a heart attack. This juice can radically improve your heart health while still tasting like a dream.

# Apple Sour

Four medium sized apples
Three large stalks of celery
One large orange, peeled
One thumbnail sized piece of ginger root
One lemon, unpeeled

Think of this juice as a new healthier twist on traditional apple juice. The celery, although perhaps not the tastiest produce, is high in vitamins and minerals that help to maintain the skin's youthful elasticity and aid complexion. Celery can also help to calm the nerves and reduce high blood pressure. The orange juice also helps to protect the skin by attacking and eliminating free radicals within the body.

# Green All Day

Two medium sized green apples (i.e. Granny Smith)
Half a medium sized cucumber
Two large stalks of celery
Three cups of parsley
One cup of spinach
One half of a lime, peeled

This juice is great for cleansing the body of toxins and facilitating enhanced liver and kidney function. The significant quantity of parsley also makes this juice a powerful immune system booster. Parsley has been shown to promote a strong immune system that keeps the whole body healthy and wards of colds, the flu, and other common ailments. Parsley is nutrient dense and provides a significant source of numerous vitamins including vitamin A, vitamin B 12, vitamin C, and vitamin K.

# Citrus Glow

Two stalks of celery
Half an English cucumber
One lemon, peeled
One medium sized Granny Smith apples (granny smith)
One medium sized pear, any variety you like
Four cups of spinach
Three leaves of kale

This juice has a bold flavor that is all its own, with the sour lemon and sweet apple packing the most punch. Even if you are not a fan of the taste of kale, you will probably still like this juice as the taste is masked by the other ingredients. This is a great juice for improving your complexion and making you feel and look vibrant and youthful. The juice from the lemon functions as a natural antiseptic that promotes skin health. The sodium in the celery is jam-packed with minerals and vitamins which promote elasticity and youthful tightness in the skin. Between the apples and the kale, you're also consuming significant quantities of vitamins A, C, E, and K, all of which prevent the appearance of premature aging by reducing free radicals in the body.

# Mango-go!

One large mango, peeled
One large orange, peeled
One lemon, peeled
Three Bartlett pears

This juice will wake you up and get you moving with it's fresh mango flavor! It also gives you a substantial dose of vitamins A, B, C, E, K, folate, niacin, riboflavin, calcium, and iron. A great way to start your day!

# Watermelon Sunshine

One third of a watermelon, rind removed
One English cucumber
Six strawberries
One cup of blueberries
Half a lime, peeled

This juice is sweet and a little high in sugar, but still has many
health benefits, such as being rich in antioxidants due to the
strawberries and blueberries. This juice is a great way to treat
yourself without feeling too guilty.

# Not Your Grandfather's Carrot Juice

Five large carrots
Half a medium sized pineapple
Two large stalks of celery
One lemon, peeled
One glove of garlic

The carrots in this juice promote a healthy cleanse by functioning as a diuretic and forcing excess fluid out of the body. In addition, the pineapple is rich in vitamins B6 and C, folate, beta carotene, and thiamin. This juice is a great way to ensure you get the recommended daily dose of potassium, magnesium, and copper. The pineapple and carrots also promote good heart health and can reduce the risk of heart disease.

# The Reset Button

One beetroot
Four cups of spinach
One teaspoon of dried spirulina
One large stalks of celery
One large carrot
One medium sized cucumber

This juice is a great choice after a weekend of indulging in alcohol. The beets in this juice works to reduce alcohol toxicity in the liver and promotes recovery by cleansing the blood and aiding in the delivering of oxygen via the bloodstream. The spinach also has cleansing properties and aids the restoration of the body's circulatory system. It has also been shown to promote brain health, which can help you recover from the mental fog a hang over faster. Finally, the calcium and magnesium in the celery stalks have been shown to ease agitation of the central nervous system.

# Beet It Clean

One beetroot
One medium sized apple
Four medium sized carrots
One cup of spinach
One large celery stalk
One cup of raspberries
Two thumb sized pieces of ginger

This juice offers a great internal cleanse. The beet juice reduces toxicity in the liver which can deliver fast relief from accidental food poisoning, diarrhea, and vomiting. It is also an excellent cure for a hangover due to the liver cleansing beetroot in the juice.

In addition to the beetroot, the apple (or apples) you use in this juice contain a natural laxative. Apple juice facilitates regular bowel movements which add to the cleansing power of this juice.

# Pink Lightning

One beetroot
Two large carrots
Three medium sized apples
One medium sized yam (sweet potato)
Two clementines, peeled

The beetroot in this juice is a great source of fast energy as your body can quickly digest the carbohydrates in the beetroot and use them to fuel your body throughout the day. This juice also facilitates proper digestion within the body and can aid indigestion. This is due to the natural laxative properties of apples. The juice in the apple promotes regular bowel movements. Carrots and beets also promote regular bowel movements by cleansing the liver and stimulating additional bile release which can aid constipation.

# Internal Scrubbing Juice

One beetroot
Three large stalks of celery
Five medium sized carrots
Thumbnail sized portion of ginger
Half a peeled lemon
One cup of spinach

When it comes to cleansing, this juice is hard to "beet". The root vegetables in this juice detoxify the liver, strengthen the blood, and aid with the reduction of any condition related to toxicity in the body, such as hepatitis, food poisoning, jaundice, and a hang over. While cleansing the body, this juice also provides an immediate energy boost that can last for hours.

# Mango Peppermint

One peeled mango
Half a medium sized cantaloupe
Ten leaves of peppermint
One thumb sized piece of ginger

This is a great tasting juice that is best enjoyed in moderation due to the sugar content and the relative lack of health benefits compared to most of the other juices in this book. Despite its status as more of a "dessert juice" it still manages to contain high levels of potassium as well as vitamins A and C. This can make it a good choice for warding off a cold or flu, as well as maintaining or improving the health of your skin, eyes, and immune system.

# Papaya Cucumber

One papaya
One medium sized peach
One clove of garlic
One medium sized cucumber
Thumbnail sized piece of ginger

This is a tasty and exotic juice that makes for a good source of vitamins A and C. It also contains plenty of antioxidants and potassium.

# Tasty Turmeric

Five thumb sized pieces or turmeric
Six medium sized carrots
One English cucumber
One medium sized apple
One large celery stalk
One medium sized pear
One thumbnail sized piece of ginger
Half a lemon, peeled

This juice is an impressive cold, flu, and fever remedy that works quickly to boost the body's immune system and fight off illness. If you are suffering from a fever in particular, consider doubling the quantity of ginger you are juicing. The lemon content in this juice facilitates perspiration while reducing feelings of nausea or dizziness. This juice also contains pears which are great for preventing a cold or flu or fighting one off by fortifying the body's immune system.

# Spinach with a Kick

Two cups of spinach
Five medium sized stalks of celery
One medium sized apple, any variety
Half of one lemon, peeled
Half of one lime, peeled
Three thumbnail sized pieces of ginger
Three cloves of garlic

Ginger isn't a flavor for everyone, but those who like it will definitely want to give this juice a try. Even those who do not like the taste of ginger may still appreciate this juice for it's effect on the digestive system. Ginger has been shown to ease digestive issues such as nausea, dizziness, motion sickness, vomiting, or an upset stomach. In fact, studies have shown that ginger is actually superior to popular prescription medication when it comes to providing relief for digestive problems!

# Orange on Orange

Six medium sized carrots
Two large oranges
Half a lime, peeled
One dash of cayenne pepper (stirred in after juicing)

This carrot heavy juice is a great way to get your daily vitamins A
and C requirement as well as loading up on beta-carotene.

# Collard Kale

Six leaves of kale
One cup of collard greens
One medium sized red bell pepper
One medium sized green bell pepper
One medium sized apple (any variety you like)
Two handfuls of cilantro
Two medium sized carrots
One medium sized cucumber

In addition to promoting overall bodily health, this juice can be an effective cancer deterrent. The collard greens are rich in nutrients that have powerful cancer fighting properties. Studies have shown both kale and collard greens can be beneficial at fighting and preventing breast cancer, prostate cancer, colon cancer, and other cancers.

This juice is also a great juice for weight loss. The kale leaves and collard greens are extremely nutrient-dense, meaning they add very few calories to this juice while still managing to deliver a significant quantity of nutrients and anti-oxidants.

# Jolly Broccoli

Two cups of broccoli florets
Two medium sized Granny Smith apples
One English cucumber
One lemon, peeled

This juice is rich in vitamins B, C, and K, as well as several important minerals. Broccoli is "nutrient dense" meaning that it is very low in calories while still being high in a variety of nutrients. Juicing with broccoli has been shown to help prevent the deterioration of eye sight due to age-related conditions like macular degeneration.

Broccoli is also a powerful cleanser and detoxifier. Some of the nutrients contained in broccoli (such as glucoraphanin, gluconasturtiin, and glucobrassicin) facilitate a natural detoxification process in the body by working to activate, neutralize, and eliminate a variety of harmful contaminants.

# Peppermint Citrus

One large pink grapefruit
One clementine (or substitute for a small orange, or half a large orange)
Six leaves of peppermint
Two cloves of garlic

This is a simple juice recipe that is easy to whip up first thing in the morning to enjoy with breakfast. It's a great way to get the day started right with a high dose of vitamin C and antioxidants to energize and strengthen the immune system. This juice is also surprisingly filling due to the grapefruit content, which makes it a great choice for a juice fast or weight loss regimen.

# Minty Red Apple

Four Red Delicious apples
Two large celery stalks
One and a half cups of mint leaves
One cup of spinach
One small lime (or half of one large lime), peeled
One quarter of a lemon, peeled

Studies have shown that consuming the juices from apples and lemons can reduce breathing difficulties, improve oxygen intake, and even prevent the development of asthma in children. The pectin found in the apples has been definitively linked to substantial reductions in "LDL" cholesterol, aka "bad" cholesterol. There is also some evidence that lemon assists with the reduction of elevated cholesterol levels as well. The vitamin C in the apples can also help to repair dry skin leaving you with skin that feels healthy and looks youthful.

# Southern Treat

One third of a medium sized pineapple
Two large stalks of celery
One medium sized cucumber
One cup of mint leaves
Half a cup of spinach
One lemon, unpeeled
One thumb sized piece of ginger

This juice has a minty flavor that combines with the ginger for an interesting kick that is sure to delight the taste buds! But this juice isn't just a great tasting, refreshing treat. The heaping amount of pineapple is dense in myriad nutrients your body needs, including vitamins B6 and C, folate, beta carotene, and thiamin. It also contains high levels of minerals like potassium, magnesium, and copper. Studies have shown that regularly consuming pineapple promotes good heart health and can reduce muscle inflammation. For this reason, this juice is great to enjoy after some physical activity.

# The Natural Fat Burner

One ruby red large grapefruit
Four medium sized carrots
One large orange, peeled
One thumbnail sized piece of ginger
One medium sized lemon, peeled
Half an English cucumber

Grapefruit is great for weight loss and maintaining a healthy heart. Studies have shown that grapefruit consumption lowers the risk of diabetes by controlling insulin production and maintaining consistent blood sugar levels, which also helps to combat obesity. The high concentration of choline, potassium, lycopene, and vitamin C in grapefruit all promote heart health and have been shown to reduce the risk of heart disease.

# A Vampire's Nightmare

Five cloves of garlic
Four stalks of celery
Four kale leaves
Three apples, any variety
One lime, peeled
Half of one lemon, peeled

Garlic in the juicer isn't for everyone, but those who like it tend to like it a lot! Garlic is highly nutritious, containing lots of maganese, fiber, selenium, calcium, copper, iron, and vitamins B1, B6, and C. Studies have shown garlic consumption can help prevent and cure the common cold. Garlic also works to lower cholesterol and blood pressure, and may aid with the prevention of certain brain diseases like Alzheimer's disease and dementia. This is probably due at least in part to the high antioxidant concentration.

# Pom-Pom Cheer

One large pomegranate
One Red Delicious apple
Four clementines, peeled
One half of a lemon, peeled
Thumb sized piece of ginger root

Pomegranates are great sources of nutrients and anti-oxidants.
Even by the standards of super foods known for their high anti-
oxidant concentration, pomegranate leaves most of them in the
dust. There is very little fat in a pomegranate and no cholesterol at
all. Pomegranate also contains lots of vitamin B5 that helps the
body metabolize the macronutrients you consume, which makes
this a great juice for anyone trying to lose some weight.

# Very Berry

One large pomegranate
One cup of raspberries
One cup of blueberries
One cup of strawberries
One medium sized pear, any variety


This juice is another tasty anti-oxidant powerhouse with a bit more sugar content due to the berries which means this is not such a great weight loss juice. It is however a great source of iron, calcium, zinc, magnesium and phosphorus. The delicious sweet taste of this juice makes it an excellent dessert. You can have a sweet treat while avoiding the many other unhealthy foods typically consumed as dessert.

# Sweet Berry Mint

Two cups of strawberries
One cup of blueberries
One cup of mint
Two large apples
One lime, peeled

This refreshing juice packs a full day's supply of vitamin C. It also has detoxifying power due to the high potassium content of the strawberries which also helps to regulate blood pressure. In addition to these benefits, strawberries are great for your mental health. Studies have shown that the folic acid found in strawberries facilitates enhanced cognition, memory, and focus. For this reason, this juice would be a perfect choice for studying or working on something that requires prolonged mental focus.

# Rock the Cabbage

Four large leaves of red cabbage
One beetroot
Three large stalk of celery
Half an English cucumber
One medium carrot
One large orange
One quarter of a pineapple
Two handfuls of spinach
Half a lemon, peeled

The pineapple flavor in this juice helps to even out the earthiness of the beetroot. If it taste too much of beet or cabbage, you can always add some extra pineapple. However you juice it though, this recipe is extremely healthy as it is jam-packed with the vitamins and minerals your body needs.

This juice is a powerful cleanser. The beet juice aids in reducing liver toxicity and combats conditions relating to bile, such as food poisoning, jaundice, hepatitis, diarrhea, and vomiting. The spinach also aids in cleansing the body, especially the intestinal tract, while its high levels of iron help to fortify the blood.

# Going Green

Two large stalks of celery
Three medium sized Granny Smith apples
One medium sized cucumber
Two handfuls of spinach
Two leaves of kale
One lemon, peeled
One half of a lime, peeled

They don't come much greener then this tasty, healthy recipe. This juice is a solid choice for anyone wanting to focus on cleansing the body of toxins. Cleansing can be an effective way to jump start a recovery after a binge on unhealthy food or toxic substances like alcohol. It can also be a great way to energize the body even when you normally eat well and live an active lifestyle. If you are doing a juice cleanse, make this drink a staple of the cleanse by drinking it either daily or every other day.

# Honeydew for You

One honeydew melon, chopped
One Bartlett pear
One apple, any variety
One handful of red grapes
One lime, peeled

Not only do honeydew melons taste great and yield lots of juice, but they are also a great source of carotenoids. Carotenoids has been shown to promote a variety of desirable health benefits including decreasing the risk of particular cancers and eye diseases. They also have protective benefits for the skin that will help you look and feel younger. Reproductive health and bone density can also improve with regular consumption of carotenoids. The grapes in this juice add a nice, complementary flavor to the melon and more than that, they also contain a variety of anti-inflammatory nutrients that promote longevity!

# Down to Earth

Two medium sized apples, any variety
Two beetroot
Four large carrots
One third of a medium sized pineapple
One thumb sized piece of garlic

Beetroot is rich in key minerals like potassium, magnesium, and iron. It also packs in high levels of vitamins A, B6 and C. In addition, it is rich in anti-oxidants and low in calories. The apple and the pineapple provide enough of a sweet flavor that the taste of beet is toned down greatly in this juice.

# Coconut Lifestyle

Two cups of fresh chopped coconut
Two medium sized carrots
Three Granny Smith apples
One clove of garlic
One thumb sized ginger

This is a great tasting juice with a noticeable sweetness that isn't overpowering. The texture is smooth and creamy, and the "zing" can be amped up by doubling the ginger content. The color is a rich and creamy orange and it provides the delicious and refreshing flavor of coconut while also containing significant nutrients and anti-oxidants that will energize the body for hours. A great juice to reinvigorate yourself after a long day at work.

# Green Be-Leaves

Five leaves of kale
One cup of spinach
Three large stalks of celery
One English cucumber
One lemon, peeled

Kale is such a healthy vegetable that you'll want to consume it as often as possible. You can cycle through the various kale recipes in this book to keep yourself from getting bored. Juices with significant kale quantity and little to no fruit, like this juice, are excellent juices for weight loss. This is because kale is extremely nutrient dense. Drinking kale juice means that you can easily get an entire day's supply of many vitamins and nutrients while hardly consuming any calories.

# Green Earth

Two beetroot
Three leaves of kale
Four leaves of Romaine lettuce
One English cucumber
Two large stalks of celery
Two large sized carrots

A delicious would-be green juice with some carrot and beet thrown in. That means that in addition to all of the health benefits of a green juice, you also get the powerful cleansing ability of beet that aids the body in purging toxins and enhancing the health of organs like the kidney and liver.

# Pear of Yams

Two medium sized pears
Two yam (sweet potato)
One large orange, peeled
Three large stalks of celery

This juice not only tastes great, it also has some impressive health
benefits as well as it is high in folate, niacin, riboflavin, and
vitamins B-6 and K. The pears are also high in boron which
prevents calcium loss and promotes bone health. The pears also
contain high levels of anti-oxidants and can fight high blood
pressure as well as reduce inflammation.

# Hawaiian Spice

One large slice of pineapple (chop if needed)
One medium sized apple (any variety you like)
Five large stalks of celery
One lemon, peeled
One thumbnail sized piece of ginger

This juice is so sweet you could have it as a dessert while still getting all the healthy benefits of juicing with fruit and vegetables. This juice is consistently a favorite for its great taste, but it can also improve your the function of your cardiovascular system. Studies have shown that consuming the juices from apples and lemons can reduce breathing difficulties, improve oxygen intake, and even prevent the development of asthma in children. The ginger in this juice will also aid in reduction of inflammation which can reduce pain and increase mobility.

# Parsnip Pumpkin Spice

Two parsnips
Four medium sized carrots
Four large stalks of celery
One lemon, peeled
Half a table spoon of pumpkin pie spice (add after juicing)

Parsnips are not commonly juiced, a fact that makes this recipe unique. If you've never tried a parsnip juice, give this one a try. There are lots of great reasons to enjoy parsnip juice as a regular part of your diet. Parsnips contain an exceptionally wide variety of various nutrients, vitamins, and minerals. Parsnips are high in folate, potassium, dietary fiber, and vitamin C.

# Strawberry Banger

Two cups of strawberries
Three medium sized apples, any variety
One lime, peeled
One lemon, peeled

Although this is still a healthy juice, it has a relatively high sugar content due to all the fruits. For this reason this juice can be a nice treat once in awhile, but not something you would want to consumer every day. That said, this juice still has some serious health benefits, such as it's detoxifying ability. Strawberries are high in potassium and promote detoxification. They also aid in regulation of the blood pressure.

# Carrot Patch Kid

Five large carrots
One English cucumber
Two medium sized Granny Smith apples
One whole lemon, peeled
One thumb sized piece of ginger root
One clove of garlic

This juice is rich in pectin and as such is a great way to combat high cholesterol. Pectin is found in both apples and carrots and has been definitively linked to substantial reductions in "LDL" cholesterol, aka "bad" cholesterol. There is also some evidence that ginger and lemon assist with the reduction of elevated cholesterol levels as well. The vitamin C in this juice which comes primarily from the carrots can also help to repair dry skin leaving you with skin that feels healthy and looks youthful.

# The Fennel Cleanse

One large cucumber
Three stalks of celery
Three medium sized Red Delicious apples
One fennel bulb and stem
One lime, peeled

A great juice to use as part of a juice cleanse due to its high water content from the cucumbers. It is also packed full of vitamins, in particular vitamin A and vitamin K, as well as a solid amount of potassium.

# Cayenne Lip Smacker

One large orange
Two large peaches
Two cups of pineapple
One lemon, peeled
One thumb sized piece of ginger
One pinch of cayenne pepper (stirred in after juicing)

This tasty juice provides all the vitamin C you need for a whole day. It is also a superb anti-cancer juice. The anti-oxidant power of the vitamin C works to rid the body of free radicals while the limioid compound in the oranges has been shown to fight a variety of different cancers including breast cancer, stomach cancer, colon cancer, and skin cancer.

# Beet Drinker

Two beetroot
Five medium sized carrots
One English cucumber
Three stalks of asparagus
Two cloves of garlic

This juice is a great way to make sure you are getting your daily recommended amount of manganese and folate as beetroot is rich in both. This juice is simple and quick to prepare, with no frills, no fruit, and nothing sweet about it. It is a good juice for when you are in a rush or don't have many fruits or vegetables handy, but don't want to skimp on your vegetable consumption.

# Emerald City

One English cucumber
Two cups of spinach
Two handfuls of parsley
Two medium sized Granny Smith apples
Two leaves of kale

This juice is as green as green can be. The apples provide a hint of sweetness that will make this drink a favorite even for people who dislike the taste of kale and spinach. The parsley in this juice will also help to reduce the gas and bloating that some people experience when juicing with raw kale. The spinach is a great intestinal tract cleanser that reduces the buildup of waste and facilitates the body's digestive system working efficiently without any digestive issues. The natural laxative found in apples also promotes regular bowel movements. This juice is also rich in vitamins and minerals that the body needs. For example, a small 15 oz glass of this juice provides an entire day's supply of vitamins C and K, as well as the mineral copper.

# The Monsoon

One cup of spinach
Two salad tomatoes
One handful of parsley
One medium sized red bell pepper
Six large stalks of celery
Half a lemon, peeled

This juice is focused on health and weight loss as it is very heavy on the vegetables as opposed to fruit. If you need an energy boost to get you through the day you can't go wrong with this juice as it is rich in both phosphorous and potassium. This juice is also a great recovery drink after a hard workout. This is due not only to the energy boost the juice delivers, but also due to its ability to reduce inflammation. Spinach is highly alkaline which can help to reduce inflammation. The tomatoes are also rich in inflammation-fighting vitamins and nutrients, many of which are contained in the skin of the tomato.

# Ruckus Juice

Four kiwi
Two cups of blackberries
One quarter pineapple
One thumb sized piece of ginger
Half a lemon, peeled

A smooth juice with just a hint of sour, this juice is always a hit
with those who love the taste of blackberries. Kiwi juice contains
high levels of antioxidants due to it's high levels of copper, iron,
and vitamins C and E. The antioxidant power of this juice
provides a boost to your immune system that can help the body to
prevent or quickly fight off colds or the flu.

# Heavy Pour Juice

Eight medium sized carrots
Two beetroot
Half a yam (sweet potato)
One Granny Smith apple

This juice is full of root vegetables that deliver a robust cleanse and reduces toxicity of the liver and improves conditions like hepatitis, food poisoning, diarrhea, vomiting, and jaundice. It is a great "reset" for your body after consuming alcohol as it cleanses the liver of the toxic alcohol it has been working to remove from your body. In addition to the cleansing power of beets, the carrots in this juice aid in the cleanse by functioning as a diuretic and forcing excess fluid out of the body.

Beets don't just cleanse the liver though, they also help to cleanse the blood, colon, and gall bladder. Within the bloodstream, the high iron content works to rebuild your red blood cell count so that your body can benefit from increased access to oxygen. In addition, the liver aids in the metabolization of fat. Keeping your liver cleansed and running efficiently promotes weight loss efficiency.

# The Burning Muscle Chiller

Two large oranges
Two medium sized carrots
One large stalk of celery
One thumbnail sized piece of turmeric
One thumbnail sized piece of ginger
One lemon, peeled
Five leaves of peppermint

Studies have widely recognized turmeric to be a powerful anti-inflammatory agent. This is because turmeric contains at least six components that have anti-inflammatory effects. Further, more recent studies indicate strong evidence that turmeric also has anti-cancer properties. Despite this, our typical diets don't contain nearly enough turmeric! Juicing with turmeric is a convenient and delicious way to make sure you avail yourself of its many health benefits.

# Peaches in a Glass

Six medium sized peaches
One half of a medium sized coconut (scoop the meat out and discard the shell)
Half a large orange

This tasty tropical juice boasts big quantities of copper, iron, potassium, phosphorus, magnesium, zinc, and selenium.

Selenium contributes to the proper function of the immune system as well as the reproductive system. Magnesium promotes a healthy bone density and together with zinc helps the body to process the macronutrients we consume and turn them into energy the body can use.

The minerals in this juice are important for a variety of important functions within the body. Copper and iron work together to improve the flow of oxygen through the bloodstream by boosting the production of red and white blood cells.

# Taiwanese Treat

Three medium sized guava
One medium clementine, peeled
One medium sized apple, any variety
One lime, peeled

Guava is not a popular fruit in many Western countries, which is really unfortunate for us! Guava is a delicious "super fruit" widely consumed in some tropical countries. It earned its reputation as a super fruit due to its high concentration of a wide variety of nutrients and its many health benefits. Among other vitamins, minerals, and nutrients, Guava is particularly rich in copper, vitamin C, lycopene, and antioxidants. If you aren't able to find guava at your local chain grocery store then try a smaller produce market, especially one that carries a variety of ethnic foods.

# Night Juice

One medium sized stalk of broccoli
One medium sized cucumber
Three large carrots
Two handfuls of parsley
Four stalks of celery
Four stalks of asparagus
Two table spoons of extra virgin olive oil (stir in after juicing)

This juice is an easy way to load up on folic acid and histamines which promote blood flow and improve circulation. This juice will give you an energetic feeling all over and beats slamming down another caffeine-laden energy drink or coffee when you're pulling an all-nighter.

# Juice is Where the Heart is

Three medium sized carrots
Two large peeled oranges
Two beetroot
One medium sized apple
One medium sized pear
One lemon, peeled
Half a lime, unpeeled

Drinking this juice daily will could lower your risk of a heart attack by up to two thirds! That is because moderate, consistent carrot consumption has been shown in studies to reduce cholesterol level by about 10 percent. High cholesterol is a leading cause of heart disease, therefore carrot consumption promotes heart health by reducing your risk of heart disease. Consuming carrots regularly also reduces your risk of a heart attack. In fact, some studies show a dramatic decrease in heart attack risk when carrot consumption is maintained over the course of a year.

# Christmas Themed Juice

Seven organic cherry tomatoes
One medium sized green bell pepper
Two cups of spinach
Two medium sized green apples
Three medium sized carrots
Ten red grapes
Two large celery stalks

The high levels of potassium and magnesium in this juice, as well
as the two cups of spinach, work together to lower elevated blood
pressure. The juice from the green bell pepper contains powerful
antioxidants that contribute to a reduction in cholesterol. This is a
great juice for boosting your immune system, lowering your
blood pressure, and losing weight.

# Cruciferous Kale Juice

Eight leaves of kale
Fist-sized crown of broccoli
One English cucumber
One medium sized apples
One medium sized pear
Two cups of spinach
One lemon

A delicious, Kale based juice that is excellent for weight loss! Kale is considered a "super food" and is ideal for weight loss due to its high concentration of nutrients and low calorie content. It is among the most nutrient-dense vegetables available and this juice makes sure you can easily consume this amazing vegetable daily. Kale is also a significant source of organo-sulfur compounds. Studies show these compounds are effective at fighting many different types of cancer. One of the many amazing qualities of kale is that it can actually contribute to a destruction of cancer cells within the body.

In addition to fighting cancer that already exists in the body, kale has also been shown to prevent cancer from occurring in the first place. The sulforaphane contents of kale has been shown to reduce the risk of cancer from occurring in the body.

This drink also contains spinach, which is another vegetable studies have shown to be effective in fighting and preventing various types of cancer. The powerful anti-oxidants contained in this vegetable contribute to the deceleration of cancerous cell production and division.

# Cruciferous Cabbage Juice

One quarter of a small head of green cabbage
Two medium sized Granny Smith apples
One cup of spinach
One thumb sized piece of ginger root
Two medium sized carrots
One stalk of celery
Half a lemon, peeled

This juice is super healthy, great for weight loss, and also helps sooth any digestive issues you may be experiencing. The natural laxative in apples can aid with constipation and promote regular bowel movements. The carrots work to cleanse the liver while stimulating a release of bile that is a key component of proper digestions. Juicing with lemon and ginger root not only adds a kick to the juice's flavor, but they also both aid in digestion by reducing gas buildup. Finally, the spinach works to cleanse the intestinal tract while promoting proper digestion.

# Sunny Skydive

Three large celery stalks
Four clementines, peeled
One apple, any red variety
One lemon, peeled
One lime, peeled
Two cups of mint leaves

This is a great juice to have before a busy day where you'll be burning up energy as it has just enough sugar in the oranges to get you energized, but not so much that you'll endure a sudden post-sugar crash. The generous helping of mint adds a unique kick to the flavor of this juice that compliments the other fruits and vegetables very well. Mint also delivers some surprising health benefits. Mint has antimicrobial properties and has also been shown to sooth a queasy stomach.

# Vampire Remedy

Three medium sized carrots
Half an English cucumber
One cup of strawberries
One cup of blueberries
One medium sized apple
Three cloves of garlic

This juice provides a powerful boost to the immune system. The carrots boost the production and efficiency of the white blood cells, which help to defend the body against a variety of infections. The high vitamin C content of the strawberries aid the body in fighting and preventing colds and the flu.

# Sargent Peppermint

One medium sized orange
Five medium sized carrots
Three medium sized apples
Two large peaches
Half a lemon, peeled
One lime, peeled
Six leaves of peppermint

This juice is smooth and tasty and packs enough carrots to
meaningfully reduce your "bad" LDL cholesterol levels by about
10 percent over time. High cholesterol is a leading cause of heart
disease, therefore carrot consumption promotes heart health by
reducing your risk of heart disease and also reducing your risk of
a heart attack. This juice can radically improve your heart health
while still tasting great.

# The Sourpuss Supreme

Three large stalks of celery
Three medium sized apples
One large orange, peeled
One thumbnail sized piece of ginger root
One lemon, unpeeled
One lime, unpeeled
Two cloves of garlic

Think of this juice is a bit of a radical (but healthier!) twist on traditional apple juice. The celery is high in vitamins and minerals that help to maintain the skin's youthful elasticity and aid complexion. Celery can also help to calm the nerves and reduce high blood pressure. The orange juice also helps to protect the skin by attacking and eliminating free radicals within the body. This juice isn't for everyone but give it a try and see if you're one of the people who love it.

# Simple Farmer

Three medium sized green apples
One medium sized cucumber
One large stalk of celery
One cup of parsley
One cup of spinach
One lime, peeled

This juice is great for cleansing the body of toxins and facilitating enhanced liver and kidney function. The significant quantity of parsley also makes this juice a powerful immune system booster. Parsley is nutrient dense and provides a significant source of numerous vitamins including vitamin A, vitamin B 12, vitamin C, and vitamin K. Parsley has been shown to promote a strong immune system that keeps the whole body healthy and wards of colds, the flu, and other common ailments.

# Citrus Throw-down

One medium sized Granny Smith apple
One medium sized pear, any variety you like
Three stalks of celery
Half an English cucumber
One lemon, peeled
Two cups of spinach
Two leaves of kale

This is a great juice for improving your complexion and making you feel and look vibrant and youthful. The juice from the lemon functions as a natural antiseptic that promotes skin health. The sodium in the celery is jam-packed with minerals and vitamins which promote elasticity and youthful tightness in the skin. Between the apples and the kale, you're also consuming significant quantities of vitamins A, C, E, and K, all of which prevent the appearance of premature aging by reducing free radicals in the body.

This juice has a bold flavor that is all its own, with the sour lemon and sweet apple packing the most punch. Even if you are not a fan of the taste of kale, you will probably still like this juice as the taste is masked by the other ingredients.

# Mango Mongoose

One large mango, peeled
Three clementines. Peeled
Ten green grapes
One lemon, peeled
One pear, any variety

This juice will wake you up and get you moving with it's fresh
mango flavor. It also gives you a substantial dose of vitamins A,
B, C, E, K, folate, niacin, riboflavin, calcium, and iron. A great
way to start your day!

# Watermelon Chill

One English cucumber
Five strawberries
One cup of blueberries
Two leaves of kale
One third of a watermelon, rind removed
One lime, peeled
Half a lemon, peeled

This juice is sweet and has many health benefits, such as being rich in antioxidants due to the strawberries and blueberries. Despite the health benefits, it is a little heavy on the sugar content, so it is not the best juice for weight loss.

# Big Carrot Bounce

Five large carrots
Half a medium sized pineapple
Three large stalks of celery
Three strawberries
One lemon, peeled
One glove of garlic

The carrots in this juice promote a healthy cleanse by functioning as a diuretic and forcing excess fluid out of the body. In addition, the pineapple is rich in vitamins B6 and C, folate, beta carotene, and thiamin. This juice is a great way to ensure you get the recommended daily dose of potassium, magnesium, and copper. The pineapple and carrots also promote good heart health and can reduce the risk of heart disease while the strawberries add to its smooth and sweet taste.

# Rope a Dope

Three large carrots
One beetroot
One cup of spinach
One teaspoon of dried spirulina
Two large stalks of celery
One medium sized cucumber

This juice let's you bounce back and after a beating – a great juice after overindulging in alcohol! The beets in this juice works to reduce alcohol toxicity in the liver and promotes recovery by cleansing the blood and aiding in the delivering of oxygen via the bloodstream. The spinach also has cleansing properties and aids the restoration of the body's circulatory system. It has also been shown to promote brain health, which can help you recover from the mental fog a hang over faster. Finally, the calcium and magnesium in the celery stalks have been shown to ease agitation of the central nervous system.

# Clean The Pipes

One beetroot
One medium sized apple
Three medium sized carrots
Two cups of spinach
One cup of parsley
One large celery stalk
One cup of raspberries
Two thumb sized pieces of ginger

This juice offers a great internal cleanse. The beet juice reduces toxicity in the liver which can deliver fast relief from accidental food poisoning, diarrhea, and vomiting. It is also an excellent cure for a hangover due to the liver cleansing beetroot in the juice.

In addition to the beetroot, the apple (or apples) you use in this juice contain a natural laxative. Apple juice facilitates regular bowel movements which add to the cleansing power of this juice.

# Pink Hijinx

One medium sized yam (sweet potato)
Three clementines, peeled
One beetroot
Two large carrots
Three medium sized apples
One thumb-sized piece of ginger

The beetroot in this juice is a great source of fast energy as your body can quickly digest the carbohydrates in the beetroot and use them to fuel your body throughout the day. This juice also facilitates proper digestion within the body and can aid indigestion. This is due to the natural laxative properties of apples. The juice in the apple promotes regular bowel movements. Carrots and beets also promote regular bowel movements by cleansing the liver and stimulating additional bile release which can aid constipation.

# The Internal Body Wash

One beetroot
Two large stalks of celery
Six medium sized carrots
Thumb sized portion of ginger
Half a peeled lemon
One cup of spinach
One medium sized Red Delicious apple

A solid choice for cleansing and detoxing. The root vegetables in this juice detoxify the liver, strengthen the blood, and aid with the reduction of any condition related to toxicity in the body, such as hepatitis, food poisoning, jaundice, and a hang over. While cleansing the body, this juice also provides an immediate energy boost that can last for hours.

# Glass Fantasy

One peeled mango
One quarter of a medium sized cantaloupe
Seven leaves of peppermint
One thumb sized piece of ginger
Half a medium sized cucumber

This is a great tasting juice that is best enjoyed in moderation due to the sugar content and the relative lack of health benefits compared to most of the other juices in this book. Despite the fact that it cracks the bottom 10% of juices in this book in terms of health benefits, it is still a much healthier choice than virtually any commercially available juice you could buy at the grocery store. It also manages to contain high levels of potassium as well as vitamins A and C. This can make it a good choice for warding off a cold or flu, as well as maintaining or improving the health of your skin, eyes, and immune system.

# Papaya My Eye-a

One papaya
One medium sized peach
Two medium sized clementines, peeled
One medium sized cucumber
Thumbnail sized piece of ginger
One lemon, peeled

This is a tasty and exotic juice that makes for a good source of vitamins A and C. It also contains plenty of antioxidants and potassium.

# Zim Zam Juice Fan

Six medium sized carrots
One English cucumber
Two medium sized pears, any variety
One large celery stalk
Five thumb sized pieces or turmeric
One thumbnail sized piece of ginger
Half a lemon, peeled

This juice is an impressive cold, flu, and fever remedy that works quickly to boost the body's immune system and fight off illness. If you are suffering from a fever in particular, consider doubling the quantity of ginger you are juicing. The lemon content in this juice facilitates perspiration while reducing feelings of nausea or dizziness. This juice also contains pears which are great for preventing a cold or flu or fighting one off by fortifying the body's immune system.

# Spinach Ginger Zing-a-linger

Two cups of spinach
One leaf of kale
Four medium sized stalks of celery
Two medium sized apples, any variety
One large orange
One lemon, peeled
One lime, peeled
Three thumbnail sized pieces of ginger
Four cloves of garlic
Pinch of cayenne pepper (add after juicing)

This juice is a powerful cleaner and aids the functioning of the digestive system. Ginger has been shown to ease digestive issues such as nausea, dizziness, motion sickness, vomiting, or an upset stomach. In fact, studies have shown that ginger is actually superior to popular prescription medication when it comes to providing relief for digestive problems!

# Ain't No Ordinary Orange Juice

Six medium sized carrots
Two large oranges, peeled
One medium sized clementine, peeled
One lime, peeled
One dash of cayenne pepper (stirred in after juicing)

This carrot heavy juice is a great way to get your daily vitamins A and C requirement as well as loading up on beta-carotene. If you're bored of traditional orange juice, try a glass of this with your breakfast and break out of your breakfast boredom.

# The Belt Cincher

Five leaves of kale
One cup of collard greens
One medium sized red bell pepper
One medium sized apple (any variety you like)
Two handfuls of cilantro
Two medium sized carrots
One medium sized cucumber
Fifteen red grapes

This juice is great for weight loss. The kale leaves and collard greens are extremely nutrient-dense, meaning they add very few calories to this juice while still managing to deliver a significant quantity of nutrients and anti-oxidants.

In addition to promoting overall bodily health and weight loss, this juice can be an effective cancer deterrent. The collard greens are rich in nutrients that have powerful cancer fighting properties. Studies have shown both kale and collard greens can be beneficial at fighting and preventing breast cancer, prostate cancer, colon cancer, and other cancers.

# Mister Cruciferous

Three cups of broccoli florets
Four leaves of kale
One large orange, peeled
Two medium sized Granny Smith apples
One English cucumber
One lemon, peeled
One lime, peeled

This juice is rich in vitamins B, C, and K, as well as several important minerals. Broccoli and kale are both "nutrient dense" meaning that they are very low in calories while still being high in a variety of nutrients. Juicing with broccoli and kale has been shown to help prevent the deterioration of eye sight due to age-related conditions like macular degeneration.

Broccoli is also a powerful cleanser and detoxifier. Some of the nutrients contained in broccoli (such as glucoraphanin, gluconasturtiin, and glucobrassicin) facilitate a natural detoxification process in the body by working to activate, neutralize, and eliminate a variety of harmful contaminants.

# Drink the Pink

One large pink grapefruit
One large orange, peeled
Four leaves of peppermint
Two cloves of garlic
One lime, peeled

An excellent weight loss juice and a fine way to get the day
started right with a high dose of vitamin C and antioxidants to
energize and strengthen the immune system. This juice is also
surprisingly filling due to the grapefruit content, which makes it a
great choice for a juice fast or weight loss regimen.

# Apple for Serious

Three Red Delicious apples
One large celery stalk
One medium sized cucumber
One cup of mint leaves
One cup of spinach
One lime, peeled
Half a lemon, peeled

Studies have shown that consuming the juices from apples and lemons can reduce breathing difficulties, improve oxygen intake, and even prevent the development of asthma in children. The pectin found in the apples has been definitively linked to substantial reductions in "LDL" cholesterol, aka "bad" cholesterol. There is also some evidence that lemon assists with the reduction of elevated cholesterol levels as well. The vitamin C in the apples can also help to repair dry skin leaving you with skin that feels healthy and looks youthful.

# Home Sweet Sunset Juice

One third of a medium sized pineapple
Five green grapes
Two strawberries
Two large stalks of celery
One medium sized cucumber
One cup of mint leaves
Half a cup of spinach
Half a lemon, peeled
One thumb sized piece of ginger

This juice promotes good heart health and can reduce muscle inflammation, making it an ideal post-workout juice. This juice has a minty flavor that combines with the ginger for an interesting kick that is sure to delight the taste buds! But this juice isn't just a great tasting, refreshing treat. The heaping amount of pineapple is dense in myriad nutrients your body needs, including vitamins B6 and C, folate, beta carotene, and thiamin. It also contains high levels of minerals like potassium, magnesium, and copper.

# Like Fat to a Flame

One ruby red large grapefruit
Four medium sized carrots
Two large stalks of celery
One thumbnail sized piece of ginger
One medium sized lemon, peeled
Half an English cucumber

Ready to burn some fat? Grapefruit is great for weight loss and maintaining a healthy heart. Studies have shown that grapefruit consumption lowers the risk of diabetes by controlling insulin production and maintaining consistent blood sugar levels, which also helps to combat obesity. The high concentration of choline, potassium, lycopene, and vitamin C in grapefruit all promote heart health and have been shown to reduce the risk of heart disease.

# The Scale Loves Kale

Four stalks of celery
Six kale leaves
Three apples, any variety
Three cloves of garlic
One lime, peeled
Half of one lemon, peeled

This juice is nutrient-dense due to all the kale leaves, making it an excellent weight loss juice. The garlic in the juice isn't for everyone, but those who like it tend to like it a lot! Garlic is highly nutritious, containing lots of maganese, fiber, selenium, calcium, copper, iron, and vitamins B1, B6, and C. Studies have shown garlic consumption can help prevent and cure the common cold. Garlic also works to lower cholesterol and blood pressure, and may aid with the prevention of certain brain diseases like Alzheimer's disease and dementia. This is probably due at least in part to the high antioxidant concentration.

# Pomegranate Influence

One large pomegranate
Two Red Delicious apples
One medium sized pear, any variety
Two clementines, peeled
One half of a lemon, peeled
Thumb sized piece of ginger root

Pomegranates are great sources of nutrients and anti-oxidants.
Even by the standards of super foods known for their high anti-
oxidant concentration, pomegranate gets top marks. There is very
little fat in a pomegranate and no cholesterol at all. Pomegranate
also contains lots of vitamin B5 that helps the body metabolize
the macronutrients you consume, which makes this a great juice
for anyone trying to lose some weight.

# Berry Gains

Half a cup of raspberries
Half a cup of blueberries
One cup of strawberries
One medium sized pear, any variety
One large pomegranate
Two medium sized clementines, peeled


This juice is another tasty anti-oxidant powerhouse with a bit
more sugar content due to the berries which means this is not such
a great weight loss juice. It is however a great source of iron,
calcium, zinc, magnesium and phosphorus.

# Berry Shareable

Three cups of strawberries
Two cups of blueberries
One cup of mint
Three large apples, any variety
One English cucumber
One lime, peeled

This refreshing juice packs a full day's supply of vitamin C. It also has detoxifying power due to the high potassium content of the strawberries which also helps to regulate blood pressure. In addition to these benefits, strawberries are great for your mental health. Studies have shown that the folic acid found in strawberries facilitates enhanced cognition, memory, and focus. For this reason, this juice would be a perfect choice for studying or working on something that requires prolonged mental focus. Make enough to share it with a friend who doesn't normally juice, almost everyone loves this recipe!

# Cabbage Potential

Four large leaves of red cabbage
One beetroot
Two large stalk of celery
One English cucumber
Three medium sized carrots
One quarter of a pineapple
Two handfuls of spinach
Half a lemon, peeled

The pineapple flavor in this juice helps to even out the earthiness of the beetroot. If it taste too much of beet or cabbage, you can always add some extra pineapple. However you juice it though, this recipe is extremely healthy as it is jam-packed with the vitamins and minerals your body needs.

This juice is a powerful cleanser. The beet juice aids in reducing liver toxicity and combats conditions relating to bile, such as food poisoning, jaundice, hepatitis, diarrhea, and vomiting. The spinach also aids in cleansing the body, especially the intestinal tract, while its high levels of iron help to fortify the blood.

# Green Movement

Five leaves of kale
Two large stalks of celery
Three medium sized Granny Smith apples
One medium sized cucumber
Two handfuls of spinach

A super green, tasty, healthy recipe. This juice is a solid choice for anyone wanting to focus on cleansing the body of toxins. Cleansing can be an effective way to jump start a recovery after a binge on unhealthy food or toxic substances like alcohol. It can also be a great way to energize the body even when you normally eat well and live an active lifestyle. If you are doing a juice cleanse, make this drink a staple of the cleanse by drinking it either daily or every other day.

# Honeydew Raindrop

One honeydew melon, chopped
One Bartlett pear
Two medium sized Red Delicious apples
Five red grapes
Five green grapes
One lime, peeled

Lots of folks love the taste of honeydew melon, but just don't make an effort to consume it regularily. Not only do honeydew melons taste great and yield lots of juice, but they are also a great source of carotenoids. Carotenoids has been shown to promote a variety of desirable health benefits including decreasing the risk of particular cancers and eye diseases. They also have protective benefits for the skin that will help you look and feel younger. Reproductive health and bone density can also improve with regular consumption of carotenoids. The grapes in this juice add a nice, complementary flavor to the melon and more than that, they also contain a variety of anti-inflammatory nutrients that promote longevity!

# Benevolent Mother Earth

Three medium sized apples, any variety
Two beetroot
Seven large carrots
One quarter of a medium sized pineapple
One thumb sized piece of garlic

An earthy but very drinkable cleansing juice! Beetroot is rich in key minerals like potassium, magnesium, and iron. It also packs in high levels of vitamins A, B6 and C. In addition, it is rich in anti-oxidants and low in calories. The apple and the pineapple provide enough of a sweet flavor that the taste of beet is toned down greatly in this juice.

# The Coconut Dance

Two cups of fresh chopped coconut
Three medium sized carrots
Two Granny Smith apples
Two medium sized clementines
One clove of garlic
One thumb sized ginger

A great juice to reinvigorate yourself after a long day at work. This is a great tasting juice with a noticeable sweetness that isn't overpowering. The texture is smooth and creamy, and the "zing" can be amped up by doubling the ginger content. The color is a rich and creamy orange and it provides the delicious and refreshing flavor of coconut while also containing significant nutrients and anti-oxidants that will energize the body for hours.

# Cruciferous Leafy Green Juice

Five leaves of kale
Five leaves of box choy
One cup of spinach
One cup of broccoli florets
Three large stalks of celery
One English cucumber
One lemon, peeled

Juicing with cruciferous vegetables means that you can easily get an entire day's supply of many vitamins and nutrients while hardly consuming any calories. Kale is such a healthy vegetable that you'll want to consume it as often as possible. You can cycle through the various kale recipes in this book to keep yourself from getting bored. Juices with significant kale quantity and little to no fruit, like this juice, are excellent juices for weight loss. This is because kale is extremely nutrient dense.

# Barefoot Picnic Juice

Two beetroot
Four leaves of kale
Three leaves of Romaine lettuce
One English cucumber
Two large stalks of celery
Four large sized carrots
One medium sized clementine, peeled

A delicious "almost green" juice with some carrot, clementine, and beet thrown in. That means that in addition to all of the health benefits of a green juice, you also get the powerful cleansing ability of beet that aids the body in purging toxins and enhancing the health of organs like the kidney and liver.

# Slammin' Yammin'!

Two medium sized pears
Two leaves of kale
One medium sized yam (sweet potato)
One large orange, peeled
Three large stalks of celery
One lime, peeled

A great juice for promoting all-around health benefits. This juice not only tastes great, it also has some impressive health benefits as well as it is high in folate, niacin, riboflavin, and vitamins B-6 and K. The pears are also high in boron which prevents calcium loss and promotes bone health. The pears also contain high levels of anti-oxidants and can fight high blood pressure as well as reduce inflammation.

# Spicy tropics

Four large stalks of celery
One large slice of pineapple (chop if needed)
One medium sized apple (any variety you like)
One lemon, peeled
One thumbnail sized piece of ginger
One table spoon of cayenne pepper (stir in after juicing)

A sweet tasting juice that is still healthy! This juice is consistently
a favorite for its great taste, but it can also improve your the
function of your cardiovascular system. Studies have shown that
consuming the juices from apples and lemons can reduce
breathing difficulties, improve oxygen intake, and even prevent
the development of asthma in children. The ginger in this juice
will also aid in reduction of inflammation which can reduce pain
and increase mobility.

# Snippity Snap Sour Spice

Two parsnips
Four medium sized carrots
Two large stalks of celery
One lemon, peeled
One lime, peeled
Half a table spoon of pumpkin pie spice (add after juicing)

An unconventional recipe that is healthy and tasty! There are lots of great reasons to enjoy parsnip juice as a regular part of your diet. Parsnips contain an exceptionally wide variety of various nutrients, vitamins, and minerals. Parsnips are high in folate, potassium, dietary fiber, and vitamin C.

# Strawberries and Spice

Three cups of strawberries
Three medium sized apples, any variety
One medium sized cucumber
Two thumb-sized pieces of ginger

Although this is still a healthy juice, it has a relatively high sugar content due to all the fruit and berry content. For this reason this juice can be a nice treat once in awhile, but not something you would want to consumer every day. That said, this juice still has some serious health benefits, such as it's detoxifying ability. Strawberries are high in potassium and promote detoxification. They also aid in regulation of the blood pressure.

## Shape Up Special

Five large carrots
One medium sized Granny Smith apple
One English cucumber
One medium sized orange, peeled
One lemon, peeled
One thumb sized piece of ginger root
One clove of garlic

This juice is rich in pectin and as such is a great way to combat high cholesterol. Pectin is found in both apples and carrots and has been definitively linked to substantial reductions in "LDL" cholesterol, aka "bad" cholesterol. There is also some evidence that ginger and lemon assist with the reduction of elevated cholesterol levels as well. The vitamin C in this juice which comes primarily from the carrots can also help to repair dry skin leaving you with skin that feels healthy and looks youthful.

# High Powered Cleansing Juice

One large cucumber
Three stalks of celery
Three medium sized Red Delicious apples
One fennel bulb and stem
One cup of spinach
One lime, peeled

A great juice to use as part of a juice cleanse due to its high water content from the cucumbers. It is also packed full of vitamins, in particular vitamin A and vitamin K, as well as a solid amount of potassium. The spinach contributes to the cleansing power of this juice as it works its way through your intestinal tract.

# Level Up Your Juice

One large orange
Three large peaches
One cup of pineapple (chopped)
One medium sized pear, any variety
One lemon, peeled
One thumb sized piece of ginger
One pinch of cayenne pepper (stirred in after juicing)

This tasty juice provides all the vitamin C you need for a whole day. It is also a superb anti-cancer juice. The anti-oxidant power of the vitamin C works to rid the body of free radicals while the liminoid compound in the oranges has been shown to fight a variety of different cancers including breast cancer, stomach cancer, colon cancer, and skin cancer.

# The Full Folate

Two beetroot
Five medium sized carrots
Two stalks of celery
One English cucumber
Two leaves of kale
Two cloves of garlic

This juice is a great way to make sure you are getting your daily
recommended amount of manganese and folate as beetroot is rich
in both. This juice is simple and quick to prepare, with no frills,
no fruit, and nothing sweet about it. It is a good juice for when
you are in a rush or don't have many fruits or vegetables handy,
but don't want to skimp on your vegetable consumption.

# The Parsley and Kale Combo

Five leaves of kale
Three handfuls of parsley
One English cucumber
Two stalks of celery
One cup of spinach
One medium sized Granny Smith apple

This juice is as green as green can be. The apple provides a hint of sweetness that will make this drink a favorite even for people who dislike the taste of kale and spinach. The parsley in this juice will also help to reduce the gas and bloating that some people experience when juicing with raw kale. The spinach is a great intestinal tract cleanser that reduces the buildup of waste and facilitates the body's digestive system working efficiently without any digestive issues. The natural laxative found in apples also promotes regular bowel movements. This juice is also rich in vitamins and minerals that the body needs. For example, a small 15 oz glass of this juice provides an entire day's supply of vitamins C and K, as well as the mineral copper.

# Fat's Worst Enemy

One cup of spinach
One salad tomato
Two handfuls of parsley
Five large stalks of celery
One medium sized red bell pepper
One lemon, peeled

This juice is focused on health and weight loss as it is very heavy on the vegetables as opposed to fruit. If you need an energy boost to get you through the day you can't go wrong with this juice as it is rich in both phosphorous and potassium.

Pair this juice with a hard workout to kick your weight loss into high gear. This juice will help you recover after tearing it up in the gym. This is due not only to the energy boost the juice delivers, but also due to its ability to reduce inflammation. Spinach is highly alkaline which can help to reduce inflammation. The tomatoes are also rich in inflammation-fighting vitamins and nutrients, many of which are contained in the skin of the tomato.

# Pumping Beet Juice

Four Brussels sprouts
One beetroot
One medium sized apple
Five medium sized carrots
Half a lemon
Two large peeled oranges

Moderate, consistent carrot consumption has been shown in studies to reduce cholesterol level by about 10 percent. High cholesterol is a leading cause of heart disease, therefore carrot consumption promotes heart health by reducing your risk of heart disease. Consuming carrots regularly also reduces your risk of a heart attack. In fact, some studies show a dramatic decrease in heart attack risk when carrot consumption is maintained over the course of a year. Drinking this juice daily will could lower your risk of a heart attack by up to two thirds!

# Lean and Leaner

One medium sized green bell pepper
One large cucumber
Two cups of spinach
Two medium sized green apples
Two Brussels sprouts
Three medium sized carrots
Twenty grapes, any variety you like
One medium sized tomato

This is a great juice for boosting your immune system, lowering your blood pressure, and losing weight. The high levels of potassium and magnesium in this juice, as well as the two cups of spinach, work together to lower elevated blood pressure. The juice from the green bell pepper contains powerful antioxidants that contribute to a reduction in cholesterol.

Some people find this drink isn't sweet enough for them. If you like it a little sweeter, simply double or even triple the number of grapes and use a slightly smaller cucumber instead.

# Cruciferous Cool Juice

One large cucumber
Six Brussels sprouts
Six leaves of kale
Two medium sized apples
Two cups of spinach
One lemon

This is a new healthy spin on a classic refreshing summer favorite, lemonade. And best of all, instead of being loaded with refined sugar like most commercial lemonades available at the grocery store, this juice is great for weight loss while still quenching your thirst with a delicious taste. It contains a significant amount of raw kale. Kale is considered a "super food" and is ideal for weight loss due to its high concentration of nutrients and low calorie content. It is among the most nutrient-dense vegetables available and this juice makes sure you can easily consume this amazing vegetable daily. Kale is also a significant source of organo-sulfur compounds. Studies show these compounds are effective at fighting many different types of cancer. One of the many amazing qualities of kale is that it can actually contribute to a destruction of cancer cells within the body. In addition to fighting cancer that already exists in the body, kale has also been shown to prevent cancer from occurring in the first place. The sulforaphane contents of kale has been shown to reduce the risk of cancer from occurring in the body.

In addition to the cancer fighting and preventing power of kale, this drink also contains spinach, which is another vegetable studies have shown to be effective in fighting and preventing various types of cancer. The powerful anti-oxidants contained in this vegetable contribute to the deceleration of cancerous cell production and division.

# Cabbage and Sprout Delight

One quarter of a small head of red cabbage
Four Brussels sprouts
Three medium sized red apples (Gala, Macintosh, etc.)
Two cloves of garlic
One cup of spinach
One thumb sized piece of ginger root
Five medium sized carrots
One lemon

If you're looking for a way to incorporate more cabbage into your diet but you aren't a big fan of the taste, this juice could be the answer you've been waiting for. This is also a great juice if you're looking to sooth any digestive issues you may be experiencing. The natural laxative in apples can aid with constipation and promote regular bowel movements. The carrots work to cleanse the liver while stimulating a release of bile that is a key component of proper digestions. Juicing with lemon and ginger root not only adds a kick to the juice's flavor, but they also both aid in digestion by reducing gas buildup. Finally, the spinach works to cleanse the intestinal tract while promoting proper digestion.

# Minty Sprouts

One large orange
Two Brussels sprouts
Two apples, any variety
One cucumber
One lemon, peeled
Two cups of mint leaves

This is a great pre-workout beverage as it has just enough sugar in the oranges to get you energized, but not so much that you'll endure a sudden post-sugar crash. The generous helping of mint adds a unique kick to the flavor of this juice that compliments the other fruits and vegetables very well. Mint also delivers some surprising health benefits. Mint has antimicrobial properties and has also been shown to sooth a queasy stomach.

# Lovely Moon Juice

Eight medium sized carrots
Two Brussels sprouts
One and a half cups of strawberries
One medium sized apple
One quarter of a lemon, peeled

This is a filling juice that provides a delicious way to get all the benefits of carrots while masking their flavor with the sweet taste of strawberries. The combination of carrots and strawberries is a favorite flavor of many people who juice regularly. In terms of health benefits, this juice provides a powerful boost to the immune system. The carrots boost the production and efficiency of the white blood cells, which help to defend the body against a variety of infections. The high vitamin C content of the strawberries aid the body in fighting and preventing colds and the flu.

# Peachy Green

Eight medium sized carrots (or six large carrots)
Six Brussels sprouts
Three medium sized apples
One medium sized orange
Three large peaches
Half a lemon, peeled

Don't be fooled by all the carrots you're juicing, the end result of this recipe is a smooth, sweet, peachy drink perfect for relaxing outside on a nice summer day. Even if you dislike the taste of carrots, it is important to consume them regularly. Regular carrot consumption has been shown to reduce "bad" LDL cholesterol levels by about 10 percent. High cholesterol is a leading cause of heart disease, therefore carrot consumption promotes heart health by reducing your risk of heart disease and also reducing your risk of a heart attack. This juice can radically improve your heart health while still tasting like a dream.

# Celery Orange Breakfast Juice

Four medium sized apples
Five Brussels sprouts
Three large stalks of celery
One large orange, peeled
One thumbnail sized piece of ginger root

Think of this juice as a new healthier twist on traditional apple juice. The celery, although perhaps not the tastiest produce, is high in vitamins and minerals that help to maintain the skin's youthful elasticity and aid complexion. Celery can also help to calm the nerves and reduce high blood pressure. The orange juice also helps to protect the skin by attacking and eliminating free radicals within the body.

# The Greener the Leaner

Two medium sized green apples (i.e. Granny Smith)
One medium sized cucumber
Two cups of parsley
One cup of spinach
Two Brussels sprouts
One half of a lime, peeled

This juice is great for cleansing the body of toxins and facilitating enhanced liver and kidney function. The significant quantity of parsley also makes this juice a powerful immune system booster. Parsley has been shown to promote a strong immune system that keeps the whole body healthy and wards of colds, the flu, and other common ailments. Parsley is nutrient dense and provides a significant source of numerous vitamins including vitamin A, vitamin B 12, vitamin C, and vitamin K.

# Citrus Sprouts

Four stalks of celery
Six Brussels sprouts
One peeled lemon
Three medium sized Granny Smith apples (granny smith)
One medium sized pear, any variety you like
Four cups of spinach
Three leaves of kale


This juice has a bold flavor that is all its own, with the sour lemon and sweet apple packing the most punch. Even if you are not a fan of the taste of kale, you will probably still like this juice as the taste is masked by the other ingredients. This is a great juice for improving your complexion and making you feel and look vibrant and youthful. The juice from the lemon functions as a natural antiseptic that promotes skin health. The sodium in the celery is jam-packed with minerals and vitamins which promote elasticity and youthful tightness in the skin. Between the apples and the kale, you're also consuming significant quantities of vitamins A, C, E, and K, all of which prevent the appearance of premature aging by reducing free radicals in the body.

# Sweet and Healthy Vitamin Juice

One large mango, peeled (or two smaller sized mangos)
One large orange, peeled
Four Brussels sprouts
Half a lemon, unpeeled
Two medium sized apples
Cayenne pepper (to taste, start with one pinch)

This juice will wake you up and get you moving with it's fresh mango flavor and cayenne pepper kick! It also gives you a substantial dose of vitamins A, B, C, E, K, folate, niacin, riboflavin, calcium, and iron. A great way to start your day!

# Loud and Proud

One third of a watermelon, rind removed
One third of a pineapple, rind removed
Two Brussels sprouts
Six strawberries
One cup of blueberries
Half a lime, peeled

This juice is consistently a favorite for it's sweet, delicious taste. Unfortunately this sweet taste comes with a relatively high amount of sugar, meaning this juice really is more of a "treat" than something you would want to enjoy daily. Despite the sugar, the juice still has many health benefits, such as being rich in antioxidants due to the strawberries and blueberries. This juice is a great way to treat yourself without feeling too guilty.

# Summer Sprouts

Half a medium sized pineapple
Six Brussels sprouts
Two large carrots
One large stalk of celery
Half of one lemon, peeled
One glove of garlic

The carrots in this juice promote a healthy cleanse by functioning as a diuretic and forcing excess fluid out of the body. In addition, the pineapple is rich in vitamins B6 and C, folate, beta carotene, and thiamin. This juice is a great way to ensure you get the recommended daily dose of potassium, magnesium, and copper. The pineapples and carrots also promote good heart health and can reduce the risk of heart disease.

# Berry Pear

One and a half cups of blackberries
Two kiwi
One quarter pineapple
One medium sized pear
Two Brussels sprouts
Five leaves of peppermint

A smooth juice with just a hint of sour, this juice is always a hit with those who love the taste of blackberries. Pear juice contains high levels of antioxidants, as does the kiwi juice due to it's high levels of copper, iron, and vitamins C and E. The anti-oxidant power of this juice provides a boost to your immune system that can help the body to prevent or quickly fight off colds or the flu.

# Back to Your Roots

Eight large carrots (or twelve medium carrots)
One beetroot
One yam (sweet potato)
Three Brussels sprouts

This juice is full of root vegetables that deliver a robust cleanse with a creamy, earthy flavor. Beet juice greatly reduces toxicity of the liver and improves conditions like hepatitis, food poisoning, diarrhea, vomiting, and jaundice. It is a great "reset" for your body after consuming alcohol as it cleanses the liver of the toxic alcohol it has been working to remove from your body. In addition to the cleansing power of beets, the carrots in this juice aid in the cleanse by functioning as a diuretic and forcing excess fluid out of the body.

Beets don't just cleanse the liver though, they also help to cleanse the blood, colon, and gall bladder. Within the bloodstream, the high iron content works to rebuild your red blood cell count so that your body can benefit from increased access to oxygen. In addition, the liver aids in the metabolization of fat. Keeping your liver cleansed and running efficiently promotes weight loss efficiency.

# The Bodybuilder's cure

Three medium sized carrots
Six Brussels sprouts
One large orange
Three large stalks of celery
Two thumbnail sized piece of turmeric
One thumbnail sized piece of ginger
Half of one lemon, unpeeled

Studies have widely recognized curcumin, a component of turmeric, as a powerful anti-inflammatory agent. In fact, turmeric contains at least five other components that also have anti-inflammatory effects. Further, more recent studies indicate strong evidence that turmeric also has anti-cancer properties. Despite this, our typical diets don't contain nearly enough turmeric! Juicing with turmeric is a convenient and delicious way to make sure you avail yourself of its many health benefits.

# Easy Living

One medium sized coconut (scoop the meat out and discard the shell)
One large oranges
Two Brussels sprouts
Four medium sized peaches

This tasty tropical juice boasts big quantities of copper, iron, potassium, phosphorus, magnesium, zinc, and selenium. These minerals are important for a variety of important functions within the body. Copper and iron work together to improve the flow of oxygen through the bloodstream by boosting the production of red and white blood cells. Selenium contributes to the proper function of the immune system as well as the reproductive system. Magnesium promotes a healthy bone density and together with zinc helps the body to process the macronutrients we consume and turn them into energy the body can use.

# Resort Remix

Two medium sized guava, or one large guava (peeled or unpeeled according to preference)
One ruby red grapefruit
One kiwi
Two Brussels sprouts
One medium sized apple, any variety

Guava is not a popular fruit in many Western countries, which is really unfortunate for us! Guava is a delicious "super fruit" widely consumed in some tropical countries. It earned its reputation as a super fruit due to its high concentration of a wide variety of nutrients and its many health benefits. Among other vitamins, minerals, and nutrients, Guava is particularly rich in copper, vitamin C, lycopene, and antioxidants. If you aren't able to find guava at your local chain grocery store then try a smaller produce market, especially one that carries a variety of ethnic foods.

# Sprouting Up

Three large carrots
Six Brussels sprouts
Two medium sized Granny Smith apples
One handful of parsley
Two stalks of celery
Five stalks of asparagus
One medium sized stalk of broccoli
One medium sized cucumber
Two table spoons of extra virgin olive oil (stir in after juicing)

Don't let the mild taste of this juice fool you, this recipe delivers a high powered boost to your libido in an otherwise subtle and unassuming juice. Studies have shown that a lack of histamines in the body can cause difficulty reaching orgasm and a lack of interest in sex. The juiced asparagus stalks are a great source of folic acid which promotes the production of libido-enhancing histamines. Parsley has also been shown to improve blood flow which can enhance sexual stimulation.

# Better Than Ever Juice

One beetroot
Four Brussels sprouts
Three cups of spinach
One teaspoon of dried spirulina
Two large stalks of celery

This juice is a great choice after a weekend of indulging in alcohol. The beets in this juice works to reduce alcohol toxicity in the liver and promotes recovery by cleansing the blood and aiding in the delivering of oxygen via the bloodstream. The spinach also has cleansing properties and aids the restoration of the body's circulatory system. It has also been shown to promote brain health, which can help you recover from the mental fog a hang over faster. Finally, the calcium and magnesium in the celery stalks have been shown to ease agitation of the central nervous system.

# Deep Cleanse Goodness

One beetroot
Four Brussels sprouts
One medium sized apple
Ten medium sized carrots
Four cups of spinach
One large celery stalk
One cup of raspberries

If you don't like the taste of beets, this may not be the juice for you (although you could always sweeten it up with an extra apple if you want to). Like the other beetroot heavy juices in this book, this one is another great internal cleanse. The beet juice reduces toxicity in the liver which can deliver fast relief from accidental food poisoning, diarrhea, and vomiting. It is also an excellent cure for a hangover due to the liver cleansing beetroot in the juice.

In addition to the beetroot, the apple (or apples) you use in this juice contain a natural laxative. Apple juice facilitates regular bowel movements which add to the cleansing power of this juice.

# What's Up Juice

One beetroot
Four Brussels sprouts
One large carrot
Two medium sized apples
One medium sized yam (sweet potato)
One large orange, peeled

This juice packs a sweet flavor in a vibrant pink liquid. The appearance is sure to impress friends with whom you'll want to share this healthy and delicious recipe. Like it's bright pink color, this juice will make you feel vibrant and energized. The beetroot is a great source of fast energy as your body can quickly digest the carbohydrates in the beetroot and use them to fuel your body throughout the day.

This juice also facilitates proper digestion within the body and can aid indigestion. This is due to the natural laxative properties of apples. The juice in the apple promotes regular bowel movements. Carrots and beets also promote regular bowel movements by cleansing the liver and stimulating additional bile release which can aid constipation.

# Sprout Cleanse

One beetroot
Six Brussels sprouts
One large sized apple, or two smaller sized apples (any variety
you like)
One large stalk of celery
Five medium sized carrots
Thumbnail sized portion of ginger
Half a peeled lemon

When it comes to cleansing, this juice is hard to "beet". The root
vegetables in this juice detoxify the liver, strengthen the blood,
and aid with the reduction of any condition related to toxicity in
the body, such as hepatitis, food poisoning, jaundice, and a hang
over. While cleansing the body, this juice also provides an
immediate energy boost that can last for hours. You can add more
lemon, ginger, or apples if you want to tweak the taste and reduce
the earthy beet flavor.

# Cantaloupe Pro Circuit

Half a medium sized cantaloupe
Three Brussels sprouts
Two peeled mangos
Ten leaves of peppermint

This is a great tasting juice that is best enjoyed in moderation due
to the sugar content and the relative lack of health benefits
compared to most of the other juices in this book. Despite its
status as more of a "dessert juice" it still manages to contain high
levels of potassium as well as vitamins A and C. This can make it
a good choice for warding off a cold or flu, as well as maintaining
or improving the health of your skin, eyes, and immune system.

# Papaya Sweetheart

Two papaya
Two peaches
One medium sized apple, any variety
Two Brussels sprouts
One clove of garlic
Thumbnail sized piece of ginger

This is a tasty and exotic juice that makes for a good source of vitamins A and C. It also contains plenty of antioxidants and potassium. Try swapping out your plain old morning orange juice for this and get your day started right.

# Fat Flaming Flu Juice

Eight thumb sized pieces or turmeric
Four Brussels sprouts
Three medium sized carrots
Three medium sized apples
Three large celery stalks
Three medium sized pears
One thumbnail sized piece of ginger
Two peeled lemons

With all of the apples and pears, this juice is a little heavy on the sugar and as such it is not the best choice for a daily juice aimed at promoting weight loss. It is however a powerful cold, flu, and fever remedy that works quickly to boost the body's immune system and fight off illness. If you are suffering from a fever in particular, consider doubling the quantity of ginger you are juicing. The heavy lemon content in this juice facilitates perspiration while reducing feelings of nausea or dizziness. This juice also contains many pears which are great for preventing a cold or flu or fighting one off by fortifying the body's immune system.

# Internal Flush

One medium sized stalk of celery
One medium sized cucumber
One medium sized apple, any variety
Four Brussels sprouts
Half of one lemon, peeled
Half of one lime, peeled
One cup of spinach
Two thumbnail sized pieces of ginger
One clove of garlic

Ginger isn't a flavor for everyone, but those who like it will definitely want to give this juice a try. Even those who do not like the taste of ginger may still appreciate this juice for it's effect on the digestive system. Ginger has been shown to ease digestive issues such as nausea, dizziness, motion sickness, vomiting, or an upset stomach. In fact, studies have shown that ginger is actually superior to popular prescription medication when it comes to providing relief for digestive problems!

# Looking Glass Juice

Ten medium sized carrots
Four Brussels sprouts
One large cucumber
One handful of cilantro
One thumbnail sized piece of ginger root
Half a lemon
Half a lime
One dash of cayenne pepper (stirred in after juicing)

This carrot heavy juice is a great way to improve your eyesight and prevent certain diseases that effect the eye. Studies have shown that a deficiency in vitamin A can impair the ability to see in dim light. This juice contains approximately 500% of the required daily dose of vitamin A which makes it ideal for boosting this crucial vitamin in those who may be deficient. The beta-carotene in this juice is also an effective way to prevent macular degeneration, a common condition that impairs sight as the body ages. Studies have shown that people who consistently consume large quantities of beta-carotene can cut their risk of macular degeneration in half.

# Cancer Fighting Pepper Juice

Five leaves of kale
One cup of collard greens
One medium sized red bell pepper
One medium sized apple (any variety you like)
Two handfuls of cilantro
Four Brussels sprouts
Five medium sized carrots

In addition to promoting overall bodily health, this juice can be an effective cancer deterrent. The collard greens are rich in nutrients that have powerful cancer fighting properties. Studies have shown both kale and collard greens can be beneficial at fighting and preventing breast cancer, prostate cancer, colon cancer, and other cancers.

This juice is also a great juice for weight loss. The kale leaves and collard greens are extremely nutrient-dense, meaning they add very few calories to this juice while still managing to deliver a significant quantity of nutrients and anti-oxidants.

# Sprouts and Broccoli

One cup of broccoli florets
Four Brussels sprouts
Three medium sized apples
Half a lemon, peeled

Most of us don't eat enough broccoli, which is unfortunate because this vegetable contains high levels of vitamins B, C, and K, as well as several important minerals. Broccoli is "nutrient dense" meaning that it is very low in calories while still being high in a variety of nutrients. Juicing with broccoli has been shown to help prevent the deterioration of eye sight due to age-related conditions like macular degeneration.

Broccoli is also a powerful cleanser and detoxifier. Some of the nutrients contained in broccoli (such as glucoraphanin, gluconasturtiin, and glucobrassicin) facilitate a natural detoxification process in the body by working to activate, neutralize, and eliminate a variety of harmful contaminants.

# Immune Boss

One large pink grapefruit
Six Brussels sprouts
One clementine (or substitute for a small orange, or half a large orange)
Half a cup of mint
Two cloves of garlic

This is a simple juice recipe that is easy to whip up first thing in the morning to enjoy with breakfast. It's a great way to get the day started right with a high dose of vitamin C and antioxidants to energize and strengthen the immune system. This juice is also surprisingly filling due to the grapefruit content, which makes it a great choice for a juice fast or weight loss regimen.

# Green Suburban Dream

Four Granny Smith apples
Three large celery stalks
Five Brussels sprouts
One and a half cups of mint leaves
One cup of spinach
One small lime (or half of one large lime), peeled
One quarter of a lemon, peeled

Studies have shown that consuming the juices from apples and lemons can reduce breathing difficulties, improve oxygen intake, and even prevent the development of asthma in children. The pectin found in the apples has been definitively linked to substantial reductions in "LDL" cholesterol, aka "bad" cholesterol. There is also some evidence that lemon assists with the reduction of elevated cholesterol levels as well. The vitamin C in the apples can also help to repair dry skin leaving you with skin that feels healthy and looks youthful.

# Re-Jucinator

Two thirds of a medium sized pineapple
One large stalk of celery
One medium sized cucumber
One cup of mint leaves
Two Brussels sprouts
One cup of spinach
Half of one lemon, unpeeled

This is a refreshing juice inspired by the beautiful tropical weather and relaxed hospitality of the Dominican Republic. It's minty flavor is sure to delight the taste buds! But this juice isn't just a great tasting, refreshing treat. The heaping amount of pineapple is dense in myriad nutrients your body needs, including vitamins B6 and C, folate, beta carotene, and thiamin. It also contains high levels of minerals like potassium, magnesium, and copper. Studies have shown that regularly consuming pineapple promotes good heart health and can reduce muscle inflammation. For this reason, this juice is great to enjoy after some physical activity.

# Heart and Healthy Living Grapefruit

One large grapefruit (any variety you like)
Four Brussels sprouts
Three medium sized carrots
One large orange
One thumbnail sized piece of ginger

Grapefruit is great for weight loss and maintaining a healthy heart. Studies have shown that grapefruit consumption lowers the risk of diabetes by controlling insulin production and maintaining consistent blood sugar levels, which also helps to combat obesity. The high concentration of choline, potassium, lycopene, and vitamin C in grapefruit all promote heart health and have been shown to reduce the risk of heart disease.

# Coconut Rich and Creamy

Two Brussels sprouts
Three medium sized carrots
One red apple (Macintosh, Pink Lady, or any other red variety
you like)
Thumbnail sized ginger
One cup of fresh chopped coconut (or substitute for coconut milk)

This is a great tasting juice with a noticeable sweetness that isn't
overpowering. The texture is smooth and creamy, and the "zing"
can be amped up by doubling the ginger content. The color is a
rich and creamy orange and it provides the delicious and
refreshing flavor of coconut while also containing significant
nutrients and anti-oxidants that will energize the body for hours.
A great juice to reinvigorate yourself after a long day at work.

# King of Cruciferous Land

Six Brussels sprouts
Four leaves of kale
Two large stalks of celery
One small cucumber (or half of one medium sized cucumber)
One medium sized pear, any variety
Half of one lime
One cup of spinach

Kale is such a healthy vegetable that you'll want to consume it as often as possible. You can cycle through the various kale recipes in this book to keep yourself from getting bored. Juices with significant kale quantity and little to no fruit, like this juice, are excellent juices for weight loss. This is because kale is extremely nutrient dense. Drinking kale juice means that you can easily get an entire day's supply of many vitamins and nutrients while hardly consuming any calories.

# Green Cheater

One beetroot
One medium sized cucumber
Three large stalks of celery
Four large sized carrots
Four Brussels sprouts
Three leaves of kale
Half a head of romaine lettuce

A delicious would-be green juice with some carrot and beet
thrown in. That means that in addition to all of the health benefits
of a green juice, you also get the powerful cleansing ability of
beet that aids the body in purging toxins and enhancing the health
of organs like the kidney and liver.

# Pear of Orange Juice

Two large oranges (peeled)
Three large stalks of celery
One medium sized apple
Three medium sized pears
Two Brussels sprouts
One yam (sweet potato)

Another tasty, creamy juice that is a big summer hit. If it is too sweet, you can add more celery and reduce the number of pears. You could also freeze the juice in popsicle molds and serve it as a refreshing treat to cool down on a hot day.

This juice not only tastes great, it also has some impressive health benefits as well as it is high in folate, niacin, riboflavin, and vitamins B-6 and K. The pears are also high in boron which prevents calcium loss and promotes bone health. The pears also contain high levels of anti-oxidants and can fight high blood pressure as well as reduce inflammation.

# Spicy Satisfaction

One large slice of pineapple (chop if needed)
One medium sized apple (any variety you like)
Three Brussels sprouts
One large cucumber
Half a lemon, peeled
One thumbnail sized piece of ginger
Half a table spoon of pumpkin pie spice

This juice is so sweet you could have it as a dessert while still getting all the healthy benefits of juicing with fruit and vegetables. This juice is consistently a favorite for its great taste, but it can also improve your the function of your cardiovascular system. Studies have shown that consuming the juices from apples and lemons can reduce breathing difficulties, improve oxygen intake, and even prevent the development of asthma in children. The ginger in this juice will also aid in reduction of inflammation which can reduce pain and increase mobility.

# Your Parsnip Special

Two parsnips
Two Brussels sprouts
Seven medium sized carrots
Three large stalks of celery
One lemon, peeled
One thumb-sized piece of ginger

Parsnips are not commonly juiced, a fact that makes this recipe unique. If you've never tried a parsnip juice, give this one a try. There are lots of great reasons to enjoy parsnip juice as a regular part of your diet. Parsnips contain an exceptionally wide variety of various nutrients, vitamins, and minerals. Parsnips are high in folate, potassium, dietary fiber, and vitamin C.

# Sweet, Right, and Tight

Three Brussels sprouts
Three cups of strawberries
One quarter of a lime, peeled or unpeeled according to taste
Two large apples

Although this is still a healthy juice, it has a relatively high sugar content due to all the fruits. For this reason this juice can be a nice treat once in awhile, but not something you would want to consumer every day. That said, this juice still has some serious health benefits, such as it's detoxifying ability. Strawberries are high in potassium and promote detoxification. They also aid in regulation of the blood pressure.

# Garlic Zest for Life

Five large carrots
One medium sized Granny Smith apple
One whole lemon, unpeeled
One thumbnail sized piece of ginger root
One clove of garlic
Four Brussels sprouts

The lemon in this juice gives a strong citrus flavor that is balanced out by the full, earthy carrot flavor that follows. The flavor is too intense for some, and can be toned down by reducing or excluding the ginger and garlic or by adding another apple.

This juice is rich in pectin and as such is a great way to combat high cholesterol. Pectin is found in both apples and carrots and has been definitively linked to substantial reductions in "LDL" cholesterol, aka "bad" cholesterol. There is also some evidence that ginger and lemon assist with the reduction of elevated cholesterol levels as well. The vitamin C in this juice which comes primarily from the carrots can also help to repair dry skin leaving you with skin that feels healthy and looks youthful.

# Green Fuel

Six Brussels sprouts
Two medium sized green apples
One fennel bulb and stem
Two large cucumbers
One lime, peeled
One half lemon, peeled
Thumb-sized piece of ginger

This is a smooth and flavorful green juice that will delight your tastebuds with a surprising hit of lime and ginger. It is an excellent diuretic juice to use as part of a juice cleanse due to its high water content from the cucumbers. It is also packed full of vitamins, in particular vitamin A and vitamin K, as well as a solid amount of potassium.

# Fuzzy Goodness

Two large oranges
Three large peaches
Two cups of pineapple
Quarter slice of lemon
Two Brussels sprouts
One pinch of cayenne pepper (stirred in after juicing)

This tasty juice provides all the vitamin C you need for a whole day. It is also a superb anti-cancer juice. The anti-oxidant power of the vitamin C works to rid the body of free radicals while the limioid compound in the oranges has been shown to fight a variety of different cancers including breast cancer, stomach cancer, colon cancer, and skin cancer.

# The Mind's Eye

Seven Brussels sprouts
Two beetroot
Three medium sized carrots
One stalk of celery
One small cucumber (or half of one medium sized cucumber)

This juice is a great way to make sure you are getting your daily recommended amount of manganese and folate as beetroot is rich in both. This juice is simple and quick to prepare, with no frills, no fruit, and nothing sweet about it. It is a good juice for when you are in a rush or don't have many fruits or vegetables handy, but don't want to skimp on your vegetable consumption.

# Greeners Gonna Green

Six Brussels sprouts
Two cups of spinach
One handful of parsley
Two medium sized Granny Smith apples
Three leaves of kale

It doesn't get much greener than this smooth, eminently drinkable juice. The apples provide a hint of sweetness that will make this drink a favorite even for people who dislike the taste of kale and spinach. The parsley in this juice will also help to reduce the gas and bloating that some people experience when juicing with raw kale. The spinach is a great intestinal tract cleanser that reduces the buildup of waste and facilitates the body's digestive system working efficiently without any digestive issues. The natural laxative found in apples also promotes regular bowel movements. This juice is also rich in vitamins and minerals that the body needs. For example, a small 15 oz glass of this juice provides an entire day's supply of vitamins C and K, as well as the mineral copper.

# Nature's Amazing Bounty Juice

One cup of spinach
One handful of parsley
Four medium sized tomatoes
One small green bell pepper (or half a medium sized green bell pepper)
Two large carrots
Two large stalks of celery
One medium sized cucumber
Two Brussels sprouts
One small lime
Salt to taste after juicing

This juice is all about health and weight loss as it is very heavy on the vegetables as opposed to fruit. If you need an energy boost to get you through the day you can't go wrong with this juice as it is rich in both phosphorous and potassium.

This juice is also a great recovery drink after a hard workout. This is due not only to the energy boost the juice delivers, but also due to its ability to reduce inflammation. Spinach is highly alkaline which can help to reduce inflammation. The tomatoes are also rich in inflammation-fighting vitamins and nutrients, many of which are contained in the skin of the tomato.

# Chard Sprouts

Four chard leaves
Four Brussels sprouts
Four kale leaves
One cucumber
Two celery stalks
One lime, peeled
Half of one lemon, peeled
Three cloves of garlic (or to taste)

Garlic in the juicer isn't for everyone, but those who like it tend to like it a lot! Garlic is highly nutritious, containing lots of maganese, fiber, selenium, calcium, copper, iron, and vitamins B1, B6, and C. Studies have shown garlic consumption can help prevent and cure the common cold. Garlic also works to lower cholesterol and blood pressure, and may aid with the prevention of certain brain diseases like Alzheimer's disease and dementia. This is probably due at least in part to the high antioxidant concentration.

# Antioxidant Cocktail

Three Brussels sprouts
One large pomegranate
Two medium sized apples
Two large oranges
One quarter of a lemon
Thumbnail sized piece of ginger root

Pomegranate's truly are a powerhouse when it comes to nutrients and anti-oxidants. Even by the standards of super foods known for their high anti-oxidant concentration, pomegranate leaves most of them in the dust. There is very little fat in a pomegranate and no cholesterol at all. Pomegranate also contains lots of vitamin B5 that helps the body metabolize the macronutrients you consume, which makes this a great juice for anyone trying to lose some weight.

# Berry Mineral Mix

One large pomegranate
One cup of raspberries
One cup of blueberries
Two Brussels sprouts
One quarter of a lemon, peeled

This juice is another tasty anti-oxidant powerhouse like the Pomegranate Power recipe also found in this book. Here the sugar content is increased due to the berries which means this is not such a great weight loss juice. It is however a great source of iron, calcium, zinc, magnesium and phosphorus. The delicious sweet taste of this juice makes it an excellent dessert. You can have a sweet treat while avoiding the many other unhealthy foods typically consumed as dessert.

# Peppermint Apple Alive

Four Brussels sprouts
Two cups of strawberries
Ten leaves of peppermint
Two large apples
Half a lemon

This refreshing juice packs a full day's supply of vitamin C. It also has detoxifying power due to the high potassium content of the strawberries which also helps to regulate blood pressure. In addition to these benefits, strawberries are great for your mental health. Studies have shown that the folic acid found in strawberries facilitates enhanced cognition, memory, and focus. For this reason, this juice would be a perfect choice for studying or working on something that requires prolonged mental focus.

# Earthy Smooth and Clean

Three large leaves of red cabbage
One beetroot
One large stalk of celery
Three medium carrots
One large orange
Two Brussels sprouts
One quarter of a pineapple
Three handfuls of spinach
Half a lemon, peeled

The pineapple flavor in this juice helps to even out the earthiness of the beetroot. If it taste too much of beet or cabbage, you can always add some extra pineapple. However you juice it though, this recipe is extremely healthy as it is jam-packed with the vitamins and minerals your body needs.

This juice is a powerful cleanser. The beet juice aids in reducing liver toxicity and combats conditions relating to bile, such as food poisoning, jaundice, hepatitis, diarrhea, and vomiting. The spinach also aids in cleansing the body, especially the intestinal tract, while its high levels of iron help to fortify the blood.

# Cleanser Advantage

Five large stalks of celery
Three Brussels sprouts
Two medium sized Granny Smith apples
One medium sized cucumber
Two handfuls of spinach
Five leaves of kale
One quarter of a lemon, peeled
One half of a lime, peeled

They don't come much greener then this tasty, healthy recipe. This juice is a solid choice for anyone wanting to focus on cleansing the body of toxins. Cleansing can be an effective way to jump start a recovery after a binge on unhealthy food or toxic substances like alcohol. It can also be a great way to energize the body even when you normally eat well and live an active lifestyle. If you are doing a juice cleanse, make this drink a staple of the cleanse by drinking it either daily or every other day.

# Melon and More

Two pears
One apple, any variety
One honeydew melon, chopped
Two handfuls of red grapes
Two Brussels sprouts

Not only do honeydew melons taste great and yield lots of juice, but they are also a great source of carotenoids. Carotenoids has been shown to promote a variety of desirable health benefits including decreasing the risk of particular cancers and eye diseases. They also have protective benefits for the skin that will help you look and feel younger. Reproductive health and bone density can also improve with regular consumption of carotenoids. The grapes in this juice add a nice, complementary flavor to the melon and more than that, they also contain a variety of anti-inflammatory nutrients that promote longevity!

# Sweetness and Sprouts

Six Brussels sprouts
Two medium sized apples, any variety
Two beetroot
Three large carrots
One third of a medium sized pineapple

There are lots of great reasons to include beets in your diet. First of all, it is rich in key minerals like potassium, magnesium, and iron. It also packs in high levels of vitamins A, B6 and C. In addition, it is rich in anti-oxidants and low in calories. Unfortunately, not everyone enjoys the taste of beetroot due to its distinct "earthy" flavor. If you are one of those people who wants to consume more beets but you just can't stand the taste, this may be the juice that solves your problem! The apple and the pineapple provide enough of a sweet flavor that the taste of beet is toned down greatly. If you find it is two sweet, you can reduce the quantity of pineapple and include some celery or cucumber instead.

# Cholesterol Obliteration

One beetroot
One medium sized orange
Five medium sized carrots
Half a lemon
Two large red apples
One medium sized clementine

Moderate, consistent carrot consumption has been shown in studies to reduce cholesterol level by about 10 percent. High cholesterol is a leading cause of heart disease, therefore carrot consumption promotes heart health by reducing your risk of heart disease. Consuming carrots regularly also reduces your risk of a heart attack. Some studies show a dramatic decrease in heart attack risk when carrot consumption is maintained over the course of a year. Drinking this juice daily will lower your risk of a heart attack.

# Green Startup Juice

Two medium sized green bell peppers
Three stalks of celery
Two cups of spinach
Two medium sized green apples
Three medium sized carrots
One medium sized clementine
Twenty-five grapes, any variety you like
One medium sized tomato

This is a great juice for boosting your immune system, lowering your blood pressure, and losing weight. The high levels of potassium and magnesium in this juice, as well as the two cups of spinach, work together to lower elevated blood pressure. The juice from the green bell pepper contains powerful antioxidants that contribute to a reduction in cholesterol.

# Cucumber Slim Down

Three large stalks of celery
Half an English cucumber
One medium sized clementine
Six leaves of kale
One medium sized apples
Two cups of spinach
Half a lemon

This juice is great for weight loss while still quenching your thirst with a delicious taste. It contains a significant amount of raw kale. Kale is considered a "super food" and is ideal for weight loss due to its high concentration of nutrients and low calorie content. It is among the most nutrient-dense vegetables available and this juice makes sure you can easily consume this amazing vegetable daily. Kale is also a significant source of organo-sulfur compounds. Studies show these compounds are effective at fighting many different types of cancer. One of the many amazing qualities of kale is that it can actually contribute to a destruction of cancer cells within the body.

In addition to fighting cancer that already exists in the body, kale has also been shown to prevent cancer from occurring in the first place. The sulforaphane contents of kale has been shown to reduce the risk of cancer from occurring in the body.

This drink also contains spinach, which is another vegetable studies have shown to be effective in fighting and preventing various types of cancer. The powerful anti-oxidants contained in this vegetable contribute to the deceleration of cancerous cell production and division.

# Apple Juice for the New World Order

One medium sized red apple (Gala, Macintosh, etc.)
One medium sized clementine
One quarter of a small head of red cabbage
Three cloves of garlic
One thumb-sized piece of ginger root
One cup of spinach
Four medium sized carrots
Half a lemon
Half a lime

This is a great juice if you're looking to sooth any digestive issues you may be experiencing. The carrots work to cleanse the liver while stimulating a release of bile that is a key component of proper digestions. Juicing with lemon and ginger root not only adds a kick to the juice's flavor, but they also both aid in digestion by reducing gas buildup. Finally, the spinach works to cleanse the intestinal tract while promoting proper digestion.

# Healthy Horizons

Two medium sized clementines
Two large oranges
One medium sized apple, any variety
One cucumber
One lemon, peeled
Two cups of mint leaves

This is a great pre-workout beverage as it has just enough sugar in the oranges to get you energized, but not so much that you'll endure a sudden post-sugar crash. The generous helping of mint adds a unique kick to the flavor of this juice that compliments the other fruits and vegetables very well. Mint also delivers some surprising health benefits. Mint has antimicrobial properties and has also been shown to sooth a queasy stomach.

# Meal Replacement Juice

Four medium sized carrots
One medium sized cucumber
One and a half cups of strawberries
One medium sized apple
One half of a lemon, peeled
Two medium sized clementines
One lime, peeled

This is a filling juice that provides a delicious way to get all the benefits of carrots while masking their flavor with the sweet taste of strawberries. The combination of carrots and strawberries is a favorite flavor of many people who juice regularly. In terms of health benefits, this juice provides a powerful boost to the immune system. The carrots boost the production and efficiency of the white blood cells, which help to defend the body against a variety of infections. The high vitamin C content of the strawberries aid the body in fighting and preventing colds and the flu.

# Feeling Fruity

Five large peaches
Two medium sized carrots
Two medium sized clementines
One medium sized apples
One medium sized orange
Half a lemon, peeled

This recipe yields a smooth, sweet, peachy drink. Even if you dislike the taste of carrots, it is important to consume them regularly and in this juice you can barely taste them. Regular carrot consumption has been shown to reduce "bad" LDL cholesterol levels by about 10 percent. High cholesterol is a leading cause of heart disease, therefore carrot consumption promotes heart health by reducing your risk of heart disease and also reducing your risk of a heart attack. This juice can radically improve your heart health while still tasting like a dream. The peaches are a bit high in sugar though so this is not a great daily juice for someone trying to lose weight.

# Passion, Fruit, and Ginger

Four medium sized apples
One English cucumber
Two stalks of celery
One large orange, peeled
Two medium sized clementines
One thumbnail sized piece of ginger root

A tasty apple juice with a ginger kick! The celery, although perhaps not the tastiest produce, is high in vitamins and minerals that help to maintain the skin's youthful elasticity and aid complexion. Celery can also help to calm the nerves and reduce high blood pressure. The orange juice also helps to protect the skin by attacking and eliminating free radicals within the body.

# Strong Juice

Four medium sized clementines
Three cups of parsley
One medium sized apple (any variety)
One medium sized cucumber
One cup of spinach
One half of a lime, peeled

This juice is great for cleansing the body of toxins and facilitating enhanced liver and kidney function. The significant quantity of parsley also makes this juice a powerful immune system booster. Parsley has been shown to promote a strong immune system that keeps the whole body healthy and wards of colds, the flu, and other common ailments. Parsley is nutrient dense and provides a significant source of numerous vitamins including vitamin A, vitamin B 12, vitamin C, and vitamin K.

# What's the Skinny?

Four stalks of celery
One peeled lemon
One peeled lime
Two medium sized clementines
Two medium sized Granny Smith apples (granny smith)
One medium sized pear, any variety you like
Four cups of spinach
Four leaves of kale

The sour lemon and sweet apple create an interesting flavor combination. Even if you are not a fan of the taste of kale, you will probably still like this juice as the taste is masked by the other ingredients. This is a great juice for improving your complexion and making you feel and look vibrant and youthful. The juice from the lemon functions as a natural antiseptic that promotes skin health. The sodium in the celery is jam-packed with minerals and vitamins which promote elasticity and youthful tightness in the skin. Between the apples and the kale, you're also consuming significant quantities of vitamins A, C, E, and K, all of which prevent the appearance of premature aging by reducing free radicals in the body.

# Multi-Vitamin Juice

Two large mango, peeled (or three to four smaller sized mangos)
Three medium sized clementines
Half a lemon, peeled
One medium sized apple

This juice adds a little twist to the fresh mango flavor everyone
loves! It also gives you a substantial dose of vitamins A, B, C, E,
K, folate, niacin, riboflavin, calcium, and iron.

# Treat Yo' Self Juice

One medium sized clementine
One quarter of a watermelon, rind removed
One quarter of a pineapple, rind removed
Four strawberries
One cup of blueberries
Half a cup of raspberries
Half a lime, peeled

This juice is consistently a favorite for it's sweet, delicious taste.
Unfortunately this sweet taste comes with a relatively high
amount of sugar, meaning this juice really is more of a "treat"
than something you would want to enjoy daily. Despite the sugar,
the juice still has many health benefits, such as being rich in
antioxidants due to the strawberries and blueberries. This juice is
a great way to treat yourself without feeling too guilty.

# Clementine Punch

Three medium sized clementines
Half a medium sized pineapple
Two large carrots
Half of one lemon, peeled
Mix with an equal part of club soda after juicing

This is a great tasting, healthy punch to enjoy at a party or with friends. The carrots in this juice promote a healthy cleanse by functioning as a diuretic and forcing excess fluid out of the body. In addition, the pineapple is rich in vitamins B6 and C, folate, beta carotene, and thiamin. This juice is a great way to ensure you get the recommended daily dose of potassium, magnesium, and copper. The pineapples and carrots also promote good heart health and can reduce the risk of heart disease.

# Pear of Kiwi

One cup of blackberries
One English cucumber
Two kiwi
One medium sized pear
One medium sized clementine
Five leaves of peppermint

A smooth juice with just a hint of sour, this juice is always a hit
with those who love the taste of blackberries. Pear juice contains
high levels of antioxidants, as does the kiwi juice due to it's high
levels of copper, iron, and vitamins C and E. The anti-oxidant
power of this juice provides a boost to your immune system that
can help the body to prevent or quickly fight off colds or the flu.

# The Yammerin Man

One yam (sweet potato)
Six large carrots
One medium sized clementine
Two beetroot

This juice is full of root vegetables that deliver a robust cleanse with a creamy, earthy flavor. Beet juice greatly reduces toxicity of the liver and improves conditions like hepatitis, food poisoning, diarrhea, vomiting, and jaundice. It is a great "reset" for your body after consuming alcohol as it cleanses the liver of the toxic alcohol it has been working to remove from your body. In addition to the cleansing power of beets, the carrots in this juice aid in the cleanse by functioning as a diuretic and forcing excess fluid out of the body.

Beets don't just cleanse the liver though, they also help to cleanse the blood, colon, and gall bladder. Within the bloodstream, the high iron content works to rebuild your red blood cell count so that your body can benefit from increased access to oxygen. In addition, the liver aids in the metabolization of fat. Keeping your liver cleansed and running efficiently promotes weight loss efficiency.

# Jack and Jill Recovery Juice

Three thumbnail sized piece of turmeric
Two large oranges
Two clementines
Four stalks of asparagus
One thumbnail sized piece of ginger

Studies have widely recognized curcumin, a component of turmeric, as a powerful anti-inflammatory agent. In fact, turmeric contains at least five other components that also have anti-inflammatory effects. Further, more recent studies indicate strong evidence that turmeric also has anti-cancer properties. Despite this, our typical diets don't contain nearly enough turmeric! Juicing with turmeric is a convenient and delicious way to make sure you avail yourself of its many health benefits.

# Immune System Strengthener

One medium sized coconut (scoop the meat out and discard the shell)
One large cucumber
One medium sized orange
One medium sized peaches
One medium sized clementine

This tasty tropical juice boasts big quantities of copper, iron, potassium, phosphorus, magnesium, zinc, and selenium. These minerals are important for a variety of important functions within the body. Copper and iron work together to improve the flow of oxygen through the bloodstream by boosting the production of red and white blood cells. Selenium contributes to the proper function of the immune system as well as the reproductive system. Magnesium promotes a healthy bone density and together with zinc helps the body to process the macronutrients we consume and turn them into energy the body can use.

# Superfruit Medley

Two medium sized guava, or one large guava (peeled or unpeeled according to preference)
One medium sized Granny Smith apple
One large cucumber
Two stalks of celery
Two leaves of kale
One kiwi

Guava is not a popular fruit in many Western countries, which is really unfortunate for us! Guava is a delicious "super fruit" widely consumed in some tropical countries. It earned its reputation as a super fruit due to its high concentration of a wide variety of nutrients and its many health benefits. Among other vitamins, minerals, and nutrients, Guava is particularly rich in copper, vitamin C, lycopene, and antioxidants. If you aren't able to find guava at your local chain grocery store then try a smaller produce market, especially one that carries a variety of ethnic foods.

# Get Up, Get Moving, Get Juicing

Two large carrots
One handful of parsley
Three medium sized Granny Smith apples
One stalks of celery
One medium sized clementine
Five stalks of asparagus
One medium sized cucumber


This recipe yields a mild tasting juice with a kick to boost your blood circulation. Studies have shown that a lack of histamines in the body can contribute to poor circulation. The juiced asparagus stalks are a great source of folic acid which promotes the production of histamines and parsley has also been shown to improve blood flow within the body.

# Synaptic Sharpener

Two beetroots
Three cups of spinach
Three large stalks of celery
One medium sized cucumber
One medium sized clementine

This juice is a great choice after a weekend of indulging in alcohol. The beets in this juice works to reduce alcohol toxicity in the liver and promotes recovery by cleansing the blood and aiding in the delivering of oxygen via the bloodstream. The spinach also has cleansing properties and aids the restoration of the body's circulatory system. It has also been shown to promote brain health, which can help you recover from the mental fog a hang over faster. Finally, the calcium and magnesium in the celery stalks have been shown to ease agitation of the central nervous system.

# Let It Out

One beetroot
Three medium sized apple
Two medium sized clementines
Four medium sized carrots
Two cups of spinach
Two large celery stalks
One cup of raspberries

This juice has a heavy, earthy flavor from the carrots and beets.
Like the other beetroot juices in this book, this one is another
great internal cleanser. The beet juice reduces toxicity in the liver
which can deliver fast relief from accidental food poisoning,
diarrhea, and vomiting. It is also an excellent cure for a hangover
due to the liver cleansing beetroot in the juice. In addition to the
beetroot, the apples you use in this juice contain a natural
laxative. Apple juice facilitates regular bowel movements which
add to the cleansing power of this juice.

# Jazzy Carrot Time

One medium sized yam (sweet potato)
One medium sized clementine
One beetroot
Two large carrot
Two medium sized apples
One medium sized clementine, peeled

This juice will make you feel vibrant and energized as it delivers a great source of fast energy. Your body can quickly digest the carbohydrates in the beetroot and use them to fuel your body throughout the day.

This juice also facilitates proper digestion within the body and can aid indigestion. This is due to the natural laxative properties of apples. The juice in the apple promotes regular bowel movements. Carrots and beets also promote regular bowel movements by cleansing the liver and stimulating additional bile release which can aid constipation.

# Tasty Toxicity Remedy

One beetroot
Two medium sized clementines
Two large sized Granny Smith apples
Four medium sized carrots
Thumb sized piece of ginger
Two large stalks of celery
One lemon, peeled

A champion cleanser! The root vegetables in this juice detoxify the liver, strengthen the blood, and aid with the reduction of any condition related to toxicity in the body, such as hepatitis, food poisoning, jaundice, and a hang over. While cleansing the body, this juice also provides an immediate energy boost that can last for hours.

# Cantaloupe Soundtrack

Half a medium sized cantaloupe
Three medium sized clementines
One peeled mango
One medium sized pear, any variety

This is a great tasting juice that is best enjoyed in moderation due to the sugar content and the relative lack of health benefits compared to most of the other juices in this book. Despite its status as more of a "dessert juice" it still manages to contain high levels of potassium as well as vitamins A and C. This can make it a good choice for warding off a cold or flu, as well as maintaining or improving the health of your skin, eyes, and immune system.

# Gentle Papaya

Two papaya
Two medium sized clementines
Three peaches
One clove of garlic
One thumb sized piece of ginger

This juice is a good source of vitamins A and C. It also contains plenty of antioxidants and potassium. If you want more of a kick, double the garlic and ginger content!

# Spin Stopper

Six thumb sized pieces or turmeric
Three medium sized pears
Two medium sized carrots
One medium sized apple
Two medium sized clementines
Three large celery stalks
One thumbnail sized piece of ginger
One lemon, peeled

This juice works to boost your immune system and can provide quick relief for cold or flu symptoms. If you are suffering from a fever in particular, consider doubling the quantity of ginger you are juicing. The heavy lemon content in this juice facilitates perspiration while reducing feelings of nausea or dizziness. This juice also contains many pears which are great for preventing a cold or flu or fighting one off by fortifying the body's immune system.

# Digestive Chill Out

Four thumb sized pieces of ginger
Three medium sized clementines
One medium sized cucumber
Two medium sized apple, any variety
Two lemons, peeled
One clove of garlic

Ginger isn't a flavor for everyone, but those who like it will definitely want to give this juice a try. Even those who do not like the taste of ginger may still appreciate this juice for it's effect on the digestive system. Ginger and lemon have both been shown to ease digestive issues such as nausea, dizziness, motion sickness, vomiting, or an upset stomach, and this juice has both ingredients in abundance! In fact, studies have shown that ginger is actually superior to popular prescription medication when it comes to providing relief for digestive problems!

# Jump Up Bouncy Juice

Eight medium sized carrots
One large cucumber
One thumb sized piece of ginger root
Two medium sized clementines
Half a lemon
Half a lime

This carrot heavy juice is a great way to improve your eyesight and prevent certain diseases that effect the eye. Studies have shown that a deficiency in vitamin A can impair the ability to see in dim light. This juice contains over 300% of the required daily dose of vitamin A which makes it ideal for boosting this crucial vitamin in those who may be deficient. The beta-carotene in this juice is also an effective way to prevent macular degeneration, a common condition that impairs sight as the body ages. Studies have shown that people who consistently consume large quantities of beta-carotene can cut their risk of macular degeneration in half.

# The Fighter Juice

Six leaves of kale
One cup of collard greens
One medium sized clementine
One medium sized green bell pepper
Three medium sized pears
Two handfuls of cilantro
Three medium sized carrots

In addition to promoting overall bodily health, this juice can be an effective cancer deterrent. The collard greens are rich in nutrients that have powerful cancer fighting properties. Studies have shown both kale and collard greens can be beneficial at fighting and preventing breast cancer, prostate cancer, colon cancer, and other cancers.

This juice is also a great juice for weight loss. The kale leaves and collard greens are extremely nutrient-dense, meaning they add very few calories to this juice while still managing to deliver a significant quantity of nutrients and anti-oxidants.

# Sweet and Sour Cruciferous Juice

One cup of broccoli florets
Two medium sized clementines
Five medium sized apples
Half a lemon, peeled
Half a lime, peeled

Most of us don't eat enough broccoli, which is unfortunate because this vegetable contains high levels of vitamins B, C, and K, as well as several important minerals. Broccoli is "nutrient dense" meaning that it is very low in calories while still being high in a variety of nutrients. Juicing with broccoli has been shown to help prevent the deterioration of eye sight due to age-related conditions like macular degeneration.

Broccoli is also a powerful cleanser and detoxifier. Some of the nutrients contained in broccoli (such as glucoraphanin, gluconasturtiin, and glucobrassicin) facilitate a natural detoxification process in the body by working to activate, neutralize, and eliminate a variety of harmful contaminants.

# Fired Up and Ready For Anything

One large pink grapefruit
Three clementines
Two leaves of kale
Half a cup of mint
Four cloves of garlic
One thumb sized piece of ginger

This is a delicious juices that packs a high dose of vitamin C and
antioxidants to energize and strengthen the immune system. This
juice is also surprisingly filling due to the grapefruit content,
which makes it a great choice for a juice fast or weight loss
regimen.

# Granny's Age Defying Remedy

Four Granny Smith apples
Two stalks of asparagus
One clementine
One medium cucumber
One cup of spinach
One lime, peeled
One lemon, peeled

Studies have shown that consuming the juices from apples and
lemons can reduce breathing difficulties, improve oxygen intake,
and even prevent the development of asthma in children. The
pectin found in the apples has been definitively linked to
substantial reductions in "LDL" cholesterol, aka "bad"
cholesterol. There is also some evidence that lemon assists with
the reduction of elevated cholesterol levels as well. The vitamin C
in the apples can also help to repair dry skin leaving you with skin
that feels healthy and looks youthful.

# Running All Night

Half a medium sized pineapple
Two medium sized clementines
Two large stalks of celery
One cup of spinach
Half of one lime, unpeeled

The pineapple in this delicious juice contains many nutrients your body needs, including vitamins B6 and C, folate, beta carotene, and thiamin. It also contains high levels of minerals like potassium, magnesium, and copper. Studies have shown that regularly consuming pineapple promotes good heart health and can reduce muscle inflammation. For this reason, this juice is great to enjoy after some physical activity.

# The Waist Chopper

One large ruby red grapefruit
One medium sized clementine
Two medium sized carrots
One medium sized orange
One thumb sized piece of ginger

Grapefruit is great for weight loss and maintaining a healthy heart. Studies have shown that grapefruit consumption lowers the risk of diabetes by controlling insulin production and maintaining consistent blood sugar levels, which also helps to combat obesity. The high concentration of choline, potassium, lycopene, and vitamin C in grapefruit all promote heart health and have been shown to reduce the risk of heart disease.

# Orange Shades

One cup of fresh chopped coconut (or substitute for coconut milk)
Three medium sized carrots
One medium sized clementine
One medium sized orange
Two medium sized apples
One English cucumber
One thumb sized ginger

This is a great tasting juice with a noticeable sweetness that isn't overpowering. The texture is smooth and creamy, and the "zing" can be amped up by doubling the ginger content. The color is a rich and creamy orange and it provides the delicious and refreshing flavor of coconut while also containing significant nutrients and anti-oxidants that will energize the body for hours. A great juice to reinvigorate yourself after a long day at work.

## The Daily Shot

Six leaves of kale
One medium sized clementine
Five large stalks of celery
One medium sized pear, any variety
Half of one lime
One cup of spinach

Kale is such a healthy vegetable that you'll want to consume it as often as possible. Juices with significant kale quantity and little to no fruit, like this juice, are excellent juices for weight loss. This is because kale is extremely nutrient dense. Drinking kale juice means that you can easily get an entire day's supply of many vitamins and nutrients while hardly consuming any calories.

# Cleaner and Leaner

One beetroot
One medium sized cucumber
Four large sized carrots
Three leaves of kale
Two medium sized apples
Two medium sized clementines

A delicious mix between a green juice and a hearty, earthy juice.
That means that in addition to all of the health benefits of a green
juice, you also get the powerful cleansing ability of beet that aids
the body in purging toxins and enhancing the health of organs like
the kidney and liver.

# Blood Pressure Regulator

Two medium sized clementines
Four large stalks of celery
One medium sized apple
Two medium sized pears
One yam (sweet potato)

This is a tasty, creamy juice that is just a little bit sweet. This juice not only tastes great, it also has some impressive health benefits as well as it is high in folate, niacin, riboflavin, and vitamins B-6 and K. The pears are also high in boron which prevents calcium loss and promotes bone health. The pears also contain high levels of anti-oxidants and can fight high blood pressure as well as reduce inflammation.

# A Juice for Autumn

Half a medium sized pineapple (chop if needed)
Two medium sized clementines
One medium sized apple (any variety you like)
Half a lemon, peeled
One thumb sized piece of ginger
Half a table spoon of pumpkin pie spice, added after juicing

This juice is so sweet you could have it as a dessert while still
getting all the healthy benefits of juicing with fruit and
vegetables. This juice is consistently a favorite for its great taste,
but it can also improve your the function of your cardiovascular
system. Studies have shown that consuming the juices from
apples and lemons can reduce breathing difficulties, improve
oxygen intake, and even prevent the development of asthma in
children. The ginger in this juice will also aid in reduction of
inflammation which can reduce pain and increase mobility.

# Parsnip Switch Up

Two parsnips
Five medium sized carrots
Two large stalks of celery
One medium sized cucumber
Two medium sized clementines
One lemon, peeled
One thumb sized piece of ginger

A tasty parsnip juice that is uncommon, but a great way to add variety to the diet of a veteran juicer. There are lots of great reasons to enjoy parsnip juice as a regular part of your diet. Parsnips contain an exceptionally wide variety of various nutrients, vitamins, and minerals. Parsnips are high in folate, potassium, dietary fiber, and vitamin C.

# Detox Treat

Three cups of strawberries
Three large apples
One medium sized clementine
One lime, peeled
One lemon, peeled


Although this is still a healthy juice, it has a relatively high sugar content due to all the fruits. For this reason this juice can be a nice treat once in awhile, but not something you would want to consumer every day. That said, this juice still has some serious health benefits, such as it's detoxifying ability. Strawberries are high in potassium and promote detoxification. They also aid in regulation of the blood pressure.

# The Big Balance

Five large carrots
One handful of parsley
One medium sized cucumber
One medium sized Granny Smith apple
Two medium sized clementines
Half a lemon, unpeeled
One thumb sized piece of ginger root
One clove of garlic

The lemon in this juice gives a strong citrus flavor that is balanced out by the full, earthy carrot flavor that follows. The flavor is too intense for some, and can be toned down by reducing or excluding the ginger and garlic or by adding another apple.

This juice is rich in pectin and as such is a great way to combat high cholesterol. Pectin is found in both apples and carrots and has been definitively linked to substantial reductions in "LDL" cholesterol, aka "bad" cholesterol. There is also some evidence that ginger and lemon assist with the reduction of elevated cholesterol levels as well. The vitamin C in this juice which comes primarily from the carrots can also help to repair dry skin leaving you with skin that feels healthy and looks youthful.

# Surprisingly Awesome

Three medium sized green apples
One fennel bulb and stem
One medium sized cucumbers
One lime, peeled
One half lemon, peeled
One thumb sized piece of ginger
Two medium sized clementines

This is a smooth and flavorful green juice that will delight your
tastebuds with a surprising hit of fennel, lime and ginger. It is an
excellent diuretic juice to use as part of a juice cleanse due to its
high water content from the cucumbers. It is also packed full of
vitamins, in particular vitamin A and vitamin K, as well as a solid
amount of potassium.

# Free Radical Exile

Two large peaches
Two medium sized clementines
Two small oranges (or one medium sized orange)
Two cups of pineapple, chopped
Half a lemon, peeled
One pinch of cayenne pepper (stirred in after juicing)

This tasty juice provides all the vitamin C you need for a whole day. It is also a superb anti-cancer juice. The anti-oxidant power of the vitamin C works to rid the body of free radicals while the limioid compound in the oranges has been shown to fight a variety of different cancers including breast cancer, stomach cancer, colon cancer, and skin cancer.

# The Fast and Folate

Two beetroot
Four medium sized carrots
One thumb sized piece of ginger
One stalk of celery
One English cucumber

This juice is a great way to make sure you are getting your daily
recommended amount of manganese and folate as beetroot is rich
in both. This juice is simple and quick to prepare, with no frills,
no fruit, and nothing sweet about it. It is a good juice for when
you are in a rush or don't have many fruits or vegetables handy,
but don't want to skimp on your vegetable consumption.

# Smooth and Flowing Free

Two medium sized clementines
Three cups of spinach
One handful of parsley
Two medium sized Granny Smith apples
Three leaves of kale
One English Cucumber

The apples provide a hint of sweetness that will make this drink a favorite even for people who dislike the taste of kale and spinach. The parsley in this juice will also help to reduce the gas and bloating that some people experience when juicing with raw kale. The spinach is a great intestinal tract cleanser that reduces the buildup of waste and facilitates the body's digestive system working efficiently without any digestive issues. The natural laxative found in apples also promotes regular bowel movements. This juice is also rich in vitamins and minerals that the body needs. For example, a small 15 oz glass of this juice provides an entire day's supply of vitamins C and K, as well as the mineral copper.

# Energy Fuel Up

One cup of spinach
One handful of parsley
One medium sized tomatoes
One medium sized red bell pepper
Three large carrots
Three large stalks of celery
One medium sized clementine
One medium sized cucumber
One lime, peeled
One lemon, peeled

This juice is all about health and weight loss as it is very heavy on the vegetables as opposed to fruit. If you need an energy boost to get you through the day you can't go wrong with this juice as it is rich in both phosphorous and potassium.

This juice is also a great recovery drink after a hard workout. This is due not only to the energy boost the juice delivers, but also due to its ability to reduce inflammation. Spinach is highly alkaline which can help to reduce inflammation. The tomatoes are also rich in inflammation-fighting vitamins and nutrients, many of which are contained in the skin of the tomato.

# Brain Booster Juice

One cucumber
Four chard leaves
Six kale leaves
Two celery stalks
One lime, peeled
One medium sized clementines
Half of one lemon, peeled
Four cloves of garlic

Garlic in the juicer isn't for everyone, but those who like it tend to like it a lot! Garlic is highly nutritious, containing lots of maganese, fiber, selenium, calcium, copper, iron, and vitamins B1, B6, and C. Studies have shown garlic consumption can help prevent and cure the common cold. Garlic also works to lower cholesterol and blood pressure, and may aid with the prevention of certain brain diseases like Alzheimer's disease and dementia. This is probably due at least in part to the high antioxidant concentration.

# Superfruit, Super Life

One large pomegranate
Three medium sized red apples (any red variety)
One large oranges
Two clementines
One half of a lemon
Two medium sized clementines
Thumb sized piece of ginger root

Pomegranate is a great source of nutrients and anti-oxidants. Even by the standards of super foods known for their high anti-oxidant concentration, pomegranate leaves most of them in the dust.
There is very little fat in a pomegranate and no cholesterol at all. Pomegranate also contains lots of vitamin B5 that helps the body metabolize the macronutrients you consume, which makes this a great juice for anyone trying to lose some weight.

# The Ironman

One large pomegranate
Half a cup of raspberries
Half a cup of blueberries
One medium sized cucumber
One medium sized clementine
One lemon, peeled
Half a small lime, peeled

This juice is a tasty anti-oxidant powerhouse and a great source of iron, calcium, zinc, magnesium and phosphorus.

# Mind Fog Dissipation

Two medium sized clementines
Three cups of strawberries
One medium sized apple, any variety
One medium sized pear, any variety
Half a lemon, peeled

This refreshing juice packs a full day's supply of vitamin C. It also has detoxifying power due to the high potassium content of the strawberries which also helps to regulate blood pressure. In addition to these benefits, strawberries are great for your mental health. Studies have shown that the folic acid found in strawberries facilitates enhanced cognition, memory, and focus. For this reason, this juice would be a perfect choice for studying or working on something that requires prolonged mental focus.

# The Circle of Life

Three large stalks of celery
Two large leaves of red cabbage
One beetroot
Two medium carrots
Two medium sized clementines
One large orange
One quarter of a pineapple
Three handfuls of spinach

The pineapple flavor in this juice helps to even out the earthiness of the beetroot. If it taste too much of beet or cabbage, you can always add some extra pineapple. However you juice it though, this recipe is extremely healthy as it is packed with the vitamins and minerals your body needs.

This juice is a powerful cleanser. The beet juice aids in reducing liver toxicity and combats conditions relating to bile, such as food poisoning, jaundice, hepatitis, diarrhea, and vomiting. The spinach also aids in cleansing the body, especially the intestinal tract, while its high levels of iron help to fortify the blood.

# Fat Burning Cleanser

Three medium sized clementines
Two large stalks of celery
Two medium sized Granny Smith apples
Two handfuls of spinach
Five leaves of kale
One lime, peeled

This juice is a solid choice for anyone wanting to focus on weight loss and cleansing the body of toxins. Cleansing can be an effective way to jump start a recovery after a binge on unhealthy food or toxic substances like alcohol. It can also be a great way to energize the body even when you normally eat well and live an active lifestyle. If you are doing a juice cleanse, make this drink a staple of the cleanse by drinking it either daily or every other day.

# The Bone Builder

One medium sized apple, any variety
One medium sized pear, any variety
Two medium sized clementines
Half a honeydew melon, chopped
One handful of green grapes

Not only do honeydew melons taste great and yield lots of juice, but they are also a great source of carotenoids. Carotenoids has been shown to promote a variety of desirable health benefits including decreasing the risk of particular cancers and eye diseases. They also have protective benefits for the skin that will help you look and feel younger. Reproductive health and bone density can also improve with regular consumption of carotenoids. The grapes in this juice add a nice, complementary flavor to the melon and more than that, they also contain a variety of anti-inflammatory nutrients that promote longevity!

# Cruisin' Along

Two beetroot
Two medium sized Granny Smith apples
Two medium sized clementines
Two large carrots
One third of a medium sized pineapple

Beetroot is rich in key minerals like potassium, magnesium, and iron. It also packs in high levels of vitamins A, B6 and C. In addition, it is rich in anti-oxidants and low in calories.

# Antioxidant Zoomer

One kiwi
One cup of cranberries
One cup of blackberries
One quarter pineapple
One medium sized pear
One thumb sized piece of ginger
Half a lemon, peeled

A smooth juice with just a hint of sour, this juice is always a hit with those who love the taste of blackberries. Pear juice contains high levels of antioxidants, as does the kiwi juice due to it's high levels of copper, iron, and vitamins C and E. The antioxidant power of this juice provides a boost to your immune system that can help the body to prevent or quickly fight off colds or the flu.

# Weight Loss Powerhouse

Six medium sized carrots
One cup of cranberries
One beetroot
One yam (sweet potato)
Two Granny Smith apples

This juice is full of root vegetables that deliver a robust cleanse and reduces toxicity of the liver and improves conditions like hepatitis, food poisoning, diarrhea, vomiting, and jaundice. It is a great "reset" for your body after consuming alcohol as it cleanses the liver of the toxic alcohol it has been working to remove from your body. In addition to the cleansing power of beets, the carrots in this juice aid in the cleanse by functioning as a diuretic and forcing excess fluid out of the body.

Beets don't just cleanse the liver though, they also help to cleanse the blood, colon, and gall bladder. Within the bloodstream, the high iron content works to rebuild your red blood cell count so that your body can benefit from increased access to oxygen. In addition, the liver aids in the metabolization of fat. Keeping your liver cleansed and running efficiently promotes weight loss efficiency.

# Celery Charge Up

One large orange
Three medium sized carrots
Two large stalks of celery
One thumbnail sized piece of turmeric
One thumbnail sized piece of ginger
Half of one lemon, unpeeled
One cup of cranberries
Five leaves of peppermint

Studies have widely recognized curcumin, a component of turmeric, as a powerful anti-inflammatory agent. In fact, turmeric contains at least five other components that also have anti-inflammatory effects. Further, more recent studies indicate strong evidence that turmeric also has anti-cancer properties. Despite this, our typical diets don't contain nearly enough turmeric! Juicing with turmeric is a convenient and delicious way to make sure you avail yourself of its many health benefits.

# Orange and Cranberries

Five medium sized peaches
One quarter of a medium sized coconut (scoop the meat out and
discard the shell)
One large orange
One cup of cranberries

This tasty tropical juice boasts big quantities of copper, iron,
potassium, phosphorus, magnesium, zinc, and selenium. These
minerals are important for a variety of important functions within
the body. Copper and iron work together to improve the flow of
oxygen through the bloodstream by boosting the production of
red and white blood cells. Selenium contributes to the proper
function of the immune system as well as the reproductive
system. Magnesium promotes a healthy bone density and together
with zinc helps the body to process the macronutrients we
consume and turn them into energy the body can use.

# Nutrient Bursting Super Juice

Two medium sized guava, or one large guava (peeled or unpeeled according to preference)
One large orange, peeled
One medium sized apple, any variety
One cup of cranberries
Half a lemon, peeled

Guava is not a popular fruit in many Western countries, which is really unfortunate for us! Guava is a delicious "super fruit" widely consumed in some tropical countries. It earned its reputation as a super fruit due to its high concentration of a wide variety of nutrients and its many health benefits. Among other vitamins, minerals, and nutrients, Guava is particularly rich in copper, vitamin C, lycopene, and antioxidants. If you aren't able to find guava at your local chain grocery store then try a smaller produce market, especially one that carries a variety of ethnic foods.

# Stimulating Jucing

Three large carrots
One handful of parsley
Four stalks of celery
Two stalks of asparagus
One medium sized stalk of broccoli
One medium sized cucumber
One cup of cranberries
Two table spoons of extra virgin olive oil (stir in after juicing)

This juice is an easy way to load up on folic acid and histamines which promote blood flow, improved circulation, and can even boost the libido! Parsley has also been shown to improve blood flow which can enhance sexual stimulation.

# Primary Health

One beetroot
Two medium sized apples
One cup of cranberries
Three medium sized carrots
Half a lemon, peeled
Half a lime, unpeeled
Two large peeled oranges

Moderate, consistent carrot consumption has been shown in studies to reduce cholesterol level by about 10 percent. High cholesterol is a leading cause of heart disease, therefore carrot consumption promotes heart health by reducing your risk of heart disease. Consuming carrots regularly also reduces your risk of a heart attack. In fact, some studies show a dramatic decrease in heart attack risk when carrot consumption is maintained over the course of a year. Drinking this juice daily will could lower your risk of a heart attack by up to two thirds!

# Potassium Popper

One cup of cranberries
Three Roma Tomatoes
One medium sized green bell pepper
Two cups of spinach
Two medium sized green apples
Three medium sized carrots
Fifteen green grapes
Two large celery stalks

This is a great juice for boosting your immune system, lowering your blood pressure, and losing weight. The high levels of potassium and magnesium in this juice, as well as the two cups of spinach, work together to lower elevated blood pressure. The juice from the green bell pepper contains powerful antioxidants that contribute to a reduction in cholesterol.

# Few Calories, Lots of Nutrients

Six leaves of kale
Half a medium sized cucumber
Three medium sized apples
One cup of cranberries
One medium sized bartlett pear
Two cups of spinach
One lemon

A delicious, Kale based juice that is excellent for weight loss! Kale is considered a "super food" and is ideal for weight loss due to its high concentration of nutrients and low calorie content. It is among the most nutrient-dense vegetables available and this juice makes sure you can easily consume this amazing vegetable daily. Kale is also a significant source of organo-sulfur compounds. Studies show these compounds are effective at fighting many different types of cancer. One of the many amazing qualities of kale is that it can actually contribute to a destruction of cancer cells within the body.

In addition to fighting cancer that already exists in the body, kale has also been shown to prevent cancer from occurring in the first place. The sulforaphane contents of kale has been shown to reduce the risk of cancer from occurring in the body.

In addition to the cancer fighting and preventing power of kale, this drink also contains spinach, which is another vegetable studies have shown to be effective in fighting and preventing various types of cancer. The powerful anti-oxidants contained in this vegetable contribute to the deceleration of cancerous cell production and division.

# Juicer's Digest

One cup of cranberries
One quarter of a small head of green cabbage
Two medium sized Granny Smith apples
One cup of spinach
One thumb sized piece of ginger root
Four medium sized carrots
One lemon, peeled

This juice helps sooth any digestive issues you may be experiencing. The natural laxative in apples can aid with constipation and promote regular bowel movements. The carrots work to cleanse the liver while stimulating a release of bile that is a key component of proper digestions. Juicing with lemon and ginger root not only adds a kick to the juice's flavor, but they also both aid in digestion by reducing gas buildup. Finally, the spinach works to cleanse the intestinal tract while promoting proper digestion.

# Running on Juice

Four clementines, peeled
Two apples, any variety
Three large celery stalks
One lemon, peeled
Two cups of mint leaves
One cup of cranberries

This is a great pre-workout beverage as it has just enough sugar in the oranges to get you energized, but not so much that you'll endure a sudden post-sugar crash. The generous helping of mint adds a unique kick to the flavor of this juice that compliments the other fruits and vegetables very well. Mint also delivers some surprising health benefits. Mint has antimicrobial properties and has also been shown to sooth a queasy stomach.

# Sneezing Be Gone

Four medium sized carrots
One cup of strawberries
Half a cup of blueberries
One cup of cranberries
One medium sized apple
One half of a lemon, peeled
Five cloves of garlic

This juice provides a powerful boost to the immune system. The carrots boost the production and efficiency of the white blood cells, which help to defend the body against a variety of infections. The high vitamin C content of the strawberries aid the body in fighting and preventing colds and the flu.

# LDL Killer

Eight medium sized carrots (or six large carrots)
Three medium sized apples
One medium sized orange
Three large peaches
One cup of cranberries
Half a lemon, peeled
Five leaves of peppermint

Don't be fooled by all the carrots you're juicing, the end result of this recipe is a smooth, sweet, peachy drink perfect for relaxing outside on a nice summer day. Even if you dislike the taste of carrots, it is important to consume them regularly. Regular carrot consumption has been shown to reduce "bad" LDL cholesterol levels by about 10 percent. High cholesterol is a leading cause of heart disease, therefore carrot consumption promotes heart health by reducing your risk of heart disease and also reducing your risk of a heart attack. This juice can radically improve your heart health while still tasting like a dream.

# Keeping It Tight

Four medium sized apples
One cup of cranberries
Three large stalks of celery
One large orange, peeled
One thumbnail sized piece of ginger root
One lemon, unpeeled

Think of this juice as a new healthier twist on traditional apple juice. The celery, although perhaps not the tastiest produce, is high in vitamins and minerals that help to maintain the skin's youthful elasticity and aid complexion. Celery can also help to calm the nerves and reduce high blood pressure. The orange juice also helps to protect the skin by attacking and eliminating free radicals within the body.

# Parsley and Cucumber Juice

Two medium sized green apples (i.e. Granny Smith)
Half a medium sized cucumber
Two large stalks of celery
Three cups of parsley
One cup of cranberries
One cup of spinach
One half of a lime, peeled

This juice is great for cleansing the body of toxins and facilitating enhanced liver and kidney function. The significant quantity of parsley also makes this juice a powerful immune system booster. Parsley has been shown to promote a strong immune system that keeps the whole body healthy and wards of colds, the flu, and other common ailments. Parsley is nutrient dense and provides a significant source of numerous vitamins including vitamin A, vitamin B 12, vitamin C, and vitamin K.

# Juice For Change

Two stalks of celery
Half an English cucumber
One lemon, peeled
One cup of cranberries
One medium sized Granny Smith apples (granny smith)
One medium sized pear, any variety you like
Four cups of spinach
Three leaves of kale


This juice has a bold flavor that is all its own, with the sour lemon and sweet apple packing the most punch. Even if you are not a fan of the taste of kale, you will probably still like this juice as the taste is masked by the other ingredients. This is a great juice for improving your complexion and making you feel and look vibrant and youthful. The juice from the lemon functions as a natural antiseptic that promotes skin health. The sodium in the celery is jam-packed with minerals and vitamins which promote elasticity and youthful tightness in the skin. Between the apples and the kale, you're also consuming significant quantities of vitamins A, C, E, and K, all of which prevent the appearance of premature aging by reducing free radicals in the body.

# Alphabet Juice

One large mango, peeled
One large orange, peeled
One lemon, peeled
Three Bartlett pears
One cup of cranberries

This juice will wake you up and get you moving with it's fresh
mango flavor! It also gives you a substantial dose of vitamins A,
B, C, E, K, folate, niacin, riboflavin, calcium, and iron. A great
way to start your day!

# Glass of Happiness and Sunshine

One third of a watermelon, rind removed
One English cucumber
Six strawberries
One cup of cranberries
One cup of blueberries
Half a lime, peeled

This juice is sweet and a little high in sugar, but still has many
health benefits, such as being rich in antioxidants due to the
strawberries and blueberries. This juice is a great way to treat
yourself without feeling too guilty.

# Beta Carotene Zinger

Five large carrots
One cup of cranberries
Half a medium sized pineapple
Two large stalks of celery
One lemon, peeled
One glove of garlic

The carrots in this juice promote a healthy cleanse by functioning as a diuretic and forcing excess fluid out of the body. In addition, the pineapple is rich in vitamins B6 and C, folate, beta carotene, and thiamin. This juice is a great way to ensure you get the recommended daily dose of potassium, magnesium, and copper. The pineapple and carrots also promote good heart health and can reduce the risk of heart disease.

# Bloody Good Juice

Two cups of cranberries
One beetroot
Four cups of spinach
One teaspoon of dried spirulina
One large stalks of celery
One large carrot
One medium sized cucumber

This juice is a great choice after a weekend of indulging in alcohol. The beets in this juice works to reduce alcohol toxicity in the liver and promotes recovery by cleansing the blood and aiding in the delivering of oxygen via the bloodstream. The spinach also has cleansing properties and aids the restoration of the body's circulatory system. It has also been shown to promote brain health, which can help you recover from the mental fog a hang over faster. Finally, the calcium and magnesium in the celery stalks have been shown to ease agitation of the central nervous system.

# Home Stomach Remedy

One beetroot
One medium sized apple
Four medium sized carrots
One cup of spinach
One large celery stalk
One cup of raspberries
One cup of cranberries
Two thumb sized pieces of ginger

This juice offers a great internal cleanse. The beet juice reduces toxicity in the liver which can deliver fast relief from accidental food poisoning, diarrhea, and vomiting. It is also an excellent cure for a hangover due to the liver cleansing beetroot in the juice.

In addition to the beetroot, the apple (or apples) you use in this juice contain a natural laxative. Apple juice facilitates regular bowel movements which add to the cleansing power of this juice.

# Keeping it Real and Regular

One beetroot
Two large carrots
Three medium sized apples
One medium sized yam (sweet potato)
Two clementines, peeled
One cup of cranberries

The beetroot in this juice is a great source of fast energy as your body can quickly digest the carbohydrates in the beetroot and use them to fuel your body throughout the day. This juice also facilitates proper digestion within the body and can aid indigestion. This is due to the natural laxative properties of apples. The juice in the apple promotes regular bowel movements. Carrots and beets also promote regular bowel movements by cleansing the liver and stimulating additional bile release which can aid constipation.

# Easy Morning

One cup of cranberries
One beetroot
Three large stalks of celery
Five medium sized carrots
Thumbnail sized portion of ginger
Half a peeled lemon
One cup of spinach

When it comes to cleansing, this juice is hard to "beet". The root vegetables in this juice detoxify the liver, strengthen the blood, and aid with the reduction of any condition related to toxicity in the body, such as hepatitis, food poisoning, jaundice, and a hang over. While cleansing the body, this juice also provides an immediate energy boost that can last for hours.

# Live to Juice

One peeled mango
One cup of cranberries
Half a medium sized cantaloupe
Ten leaves of peppermint
One thumb sized piece of ginger

This is a great tasting juice that is best enjoyed in moderation due to the sugar content and the relative lack of health benefits compared to most of the other juices in this book. Despite its status as more of a "dessert juice" it still manages to contain high levels of potassium as well as vitamins A and C. This can make it a good choice for warding off a cold or flu, as well as maintaining or improving the health of your skin, eyes, and immune system.

# Cranberry Cucumber Surprise

Two cups of cranberries
One papaya
One medium sized peach
One clove of garlic
One medium sized cucumber
Thumbnail sized piece of ginger

This is a tasty and exotic juice that makes for a good source of
vitamins A and C. It also contains plenty of antioxidants and
potassium.

# Fever Cool Down

One cup of cranberries
Five thumb sized pieces or turmeric
Six medium sized carrots
One English cucumber
One medium sized apple
One large celery stalk
One medium sized pear
One thumbnail sized piece of ginger
Half a lemon, peeled

This juice is an impressive cold, flu, and fever remedy that works quickly to boost the body's immune system and fight off illness. If you are suffering from a fever in particular, consider doubling the quantity of ginger you are juicing. The lemon content in this juice facilitates perspiration while reducing feelings of nausea or dizziness. This juice also contains pears which are great for preventing a cold or flu or fighting one off by fortifying the body's immune system.

# Flat Footed

Two cups of spinach
Five medium sized stalks of celery
One medium sized apple, any variety
Half of one lemon, peeled
Half of one lime, peeled
One cup of cranberries
Three thumbnail sized pieces of ginger
Three cloves of garlic

Ginger isn't a flavor for everyone, but those who like it will definitely want to give this juice a try. Even those who do not like the taste of ginger may still appreciate this juice for it's effect on the digestive system. Ginger has been shown to ease digestive issues such as nausea, dizziness, motion sickness, vomiting, or an upset stomach. In fact, studies have shown that ginger is actually superior to popular prescription medication when it comes to providing relief for digestive problems!

# On Solid Ground

One cup of cranberries
Six medium sized carrots
Two large oranges
Half a lime, peeled
One dash of cayenne pepper (stirred in after juicing)

This carrot heavy juice is a great way to get your daily vitamins A and C requirement as well as loading up on beta-carotene.

# Prevention and Weight Loss Juice

Six leaves of kale
One cup of collard greens
One medium sized red bell pepper
One medium sized green bell pepper
One medium sized apple (any variety you like)
One cup of cranberries
Two handfuls of cilantro
Two medium sized carrots
One medium sized cucumber

In addition to promoting overall bodily health, this juice can be an effective cancer deterrent. The collard greens are rich in nutrients that have powerful cancer fighting properties. Studies have shown both kale and collard greens can be beneficial at fighting and preventing breast cancer, prostate cancer, colon cancer, and other cancers.

This juice is also a great juice for weight loss. The kale leaves and collard greens are extremely nutrient-dense, meaning they add very few calories to this juice while still managing to deliver a significant quantity of nutrients and anti-oxidants.

# Full Body Flush

Two cups of broccoli florets
One cup of cranberries
Two medium sized Granny Smith apples
One English cucumber
One lemon, peeled

This juice is rich in vitamins B, C, and K, as well as several important minerals. Broccoli is "nutrient dense" meaning that it is very low in calories while still being high in a variety of nutrients. Juicing with broccoli has been shown to help prevent the deterioration of eye sight due to age-related conditions like macular degeneration.

Broccoli is also a powerful cleanser and detoxifier. Some of the nutrients contained in broccoli (such as glucoraphanin, gluconasturtiin, and glucobrassicin) facilitate a natural detoxification process in the body by working to activate, neutralize, and eliminate a variety of harmful contaminants.

# Fast and Juicy

One large pink grapefruit
One medium sized orange
One cup of cranberries
Six leaves of peppermint
Two cloves of garlic

This is a simple juice recipe that is easy to whip up first thing in
the morning to enjoy with breakfast. It's a great way to get the day
started right with a high dose of vitamin C and antioxidants to
energize and strengthen the immune system. This juice is also
surprisingly filling due to the grapefruit content, which makes it a
great choice for a juice fast or weight loss regimen.

# Breathing Easy

Four Red Delicious apples
One cup of cranberries
Two large celery stalks
One and a half cups of mint leaves
One cup of spinach
One small lime (or half of one large lime), peeled
One quarter of a lemon, peeled

Studies have shown that consuming the juices from apples and lemons can reduce breathing difficulties, improve oxygen intake, and even prevent the development of asthma in children. The pectin found in the apples has been definitively linked to substantial reductions in "LDL" cholesterol, aka "bad" cholesterol. There is also some evidence that lemon assists with the reduction of elevated cholesterol levels as well. The vitamin C in the apples can also help to repair dry skin leaving you with skin that feels healthy and looks youthful.

# The Southern Strategy

One third of a medium sized pineapple
Two large stalks of celery
One medium sized cucumber
One cup of mint leaves
Half a cup of spinach
One lemon, unpeeled
One cup of cranberries
One thumb sized piece of ginger

This juice has a minty flavor that combines with the ginger for an interesting kick that is sure to delight the taste buds! But this juice isn't just a great tasting, refreshing treat. The heaping amount of pineapple is dense in myriad nutrients your body needs, including vitamins B6 and C, folate, beta carotene, and thiamin. It also contains high levels of minerals like potassium, magnesium, and copper. Studies have shown that regularly consuming pineapple promotes good heart health and can reduce muscle inflammation. For this reason, this juice is great to enjoy after some physical activity.

# Close to the Heart

One ruby red large grapefruit
Four medium sized carrots
One large orange, peeled
One cup of cranberries
One thumbnail sized piece of ginger
One medium sized lemon, peeled
Half an English cucumber

Grapefruit is great for weight loss and maintaining a healthy heart. Studies have shown that grapefruit consumption lowers the risk of diabetes by controlling insulin production and maintaining consistent blood sugar levels, which also helps to combat obesity. The high concentration of choline, potassium, lycopene, and vitamin C in grapefruit all promote heart health and have been shown to reduce the risk of heart disease.

# Juicing for the Long Haul

Five cloves of garlic
Four stalks of celery
Four kale leaves
Three apples, any variety
One lime, peeled
Half of one lemon, peeled
One cup of cranberries

Garlic in the juicer isn't for everyone, but those who like it tend to like it a lot! Garlic is highly nutritious, containing lots of maganese, fiber, selenium, calcium, copper, iron, and vitamins B1, B6, and C. Studies have shown garlic consumption can help prevent and cure the common cold. Garlic also works to lower cholesterol and blood pressure, and may aid with the prevention of certain brain diseases like Alzheimer's disease and dementia. This is probably due at least in part to the high antioxidant concentration.

# Moving Forward

One large pomegranate
One Red Delicious apple
Four clementines, peeled
One cup of cranberries
One half of a lemon, peeled
Thumb sized piece of ginger root

Pomegranates are great sources of nutrients and anti-oxidants. Even by the standards of super foods known for their high anti-oxidant concentration, pomegranate leaves most of them in the dust. There is very little fat in a pomegranate and no cholesterol at all. Pomegranate also contains lots of vitamin B5 that helps the body metabolize the macronutrients you consume, which makes this a great juice for anyone trying to lose some weight.

# Merry Berry Smash

One large pomegranate
One cup of cranberries
One cup of raspberries
One cup of blueberries
One cup of strawberries
One medium sized pear, any variety


This juice is another tasty anti-oxidant powerhouse with a bit more sugar content due to the berries which means this is not such a great weight loss juice. It is however a great source of iron, calcium, zinc, magnesium and phosphorus. The delicious sweet taste of this juice makes it an excellent dessert. You can have a sweet treat while avoiding the many other unhealthy foods typically consumed as dessert.

# Berry Overtime

One cup of cranberries
One cup of strawberries
One cup of blueberries
One cup of mint
Two large apples
One lime, peeled

This refreshing juice packs a full day's supply of vitamin C. It also has detoxifying power due to the high potassium content of the strawberries which also helps to regulate blood pressure. In addition to these benefits, strawberries are great for your mental health. Studies have shown that the folic acid found in strawberries facilitates enhanced cognition, memory, and focus. For this reason, this juice would be a perfect choice for studying or working on something that requires prolonged mental focus.

# Cruciferous Veg and Berry Juice

Four large leaves of red cabbage
One beetroot
One cup of cranberries
Three large stalk of celery
Half an English cucumber
One medium carrot
One large orange
One quarter of a pineapple
Two handfuls of spinach
Half a lemon, peeled

The pineapple flavor in this juice helps to even out the earthiness of the beetroot. If it taste too much of beet or cabbage, you can always add some extra pineapple. However you juice it though, this recipe is extremely healthy as it is jam-packed with the vitamins and minerals your body needs.

This juice is a powerful cleanser. The beet juice aids in reducing liver toxicity and combats conditions relating to bile, such as food poisoning, jaundice, hepatitis, diarrhea, and vomiting. The spinach also aids in cleansing the body, especially the intestinal tract, while its high levels of iron help to fortify the blood.

# The Toxin Trim

Two large stalks of celery
Three medium sized Granny Smith apples
One cup of cranberries
One medium sized cucumber
Two handfuls of spinach
Two leaves of kale
One lemon, peeled
One half of a lime, peeled

They don't come much greener then this tasty, healthy recipe. This juice is a solid choice for anyone wanting to focus on cleansing the body of toxins. Cleansing can be an effective way to jump start a recovery after a binge on unhealthy food or toxic substances like alcohol. It can also be a great way to energize the body even when you normally eat well and live an active lifestyle. If you are doing a juice cleanse, make this drink a staple of the cleanse by drinking it either daily or every other day.

# Longevity Juice

One honeydew melon, chopped
One Bartlett pear
One apple, any variety
One handful of red grapes
One lime, peeled
One cup of cranberries

Not only do honeydew melons taste great and yield lots of juice, but they are also a great source of carotenoids. Carotenoids has been shown to promote a variety of desirable health benefits including decreasing the risk of particular cancers and eye diseases. They also have protective benefits for the skin that will help you look and feel younger. Reproductive health and bone density can also improve with regular consumption of carotenoids. The grapes in this juice add a nice, complementary flavor to the melon and more than that, they also contain a variety of anti-inflammatory nutrients that promote longevity!

# Potassium, Magnesium, and Iron, Oh My!

Two medium sized apples, any variety
Two beetroot
Four large carrots
One cup of cranberries
One third of a medium sized pineapple
One thumb sized piece of garlic

Beetroot is rich in key minerals like potassium, magnesium, and iron. It also packs in high levels of vitamins A, B6 and C. In addition, it is rich in anti-oxidants and low in calories. The apple and the pineapple provide enough of a sweet flavor that the taste of beet is toned down greatly in this juice.

# Living Off the Land

Two cups of fresh chopped coconut
Two medium sized carrots
Three Granny Smith apples
One cup of cranberries
One clove of garlic
One thumb sized ginger

This is a great tasting juice with a noticeable sweetness that isn't overpowering. The texture is smooth and creamy, and the "zing" can be amped up by doubling the ginger content. The color is a rich and creamy orange and it provides the delicious and refreshing flavor of coconut while also containing significant nutrients and anti-oxidants that will energize the body for hours. A great juice to reinvigorate yourself after a long day at work.

# Killer Kale Cocktail

Seven leaves of kale
One cup of cranberries
One cup of spinach
Three large stalks of celery
One English cucumber
One lemon, peeled

Kale is such a healthy vegetable that you'll want to consume it as often as possible. You can cycle through the various kale recipes in this book to keep yourself from getting bored. Juices with significant kale quantity and little to no fruit, like this juice, are excellent juices for weight loss. This is because kale is extremely nutrient dense. Drinking kale juice means that you can easily get an entire day's supply of many vitamins and nutrients while hardly consuming any calories.

# Green Crossing

Two beetroot
Three leaves of kale
Four leaves of Romaine lettuce
One English cucumber
Two large stalks of celery
One cup of cranberries
Two large sized carrots

A delicious would-be green juice with some carrot and beet thrown in. That means that in addition to all of the health benefits of a green juice, you also get the powerful cleansing ability of beet that aids the body in purging toxins and enhancing the health of organs like the kidney and liver.

# Don't Call Me Boron

Two medium sized pears
Two yam (sweet potato)
One large orange, peeled
Three large stalks of celery
One cup of cranberries

This juice not only tastes great, it also has some impressive health benefits as well as it is high in folate, niacin, riboflavin, and vitamins B-6 and K. The pears are also high in boron which prevents calcium loss and promotes bone health. The pears also contain high levels of anti-oxidants and can fight high blood pressure as well as reduce inflammation.

# Cardiovascular Tuneup

One large slice of pineapple (chop if needed)
One medium sized apple (any variety you like)
Five large stalks of celery
One lemon, peeled
One thumbnail sized piece of ginger
One cup of cranberries

This juice is so sweet you could have it as a dessert while still getting all the healthy benefits of juicing with fruit and vegetables. This juice is consistently a favorite for its great taste, but it can also improve your the function of your cardiovascular system. Studies have shown that consuming the juices from apples and lemons can reduce breathing difficulties, improve oxygen intake, and even prevent the development of asthma in children. The ginger in this juice will also aid in reduction of inflammation which can reduce pain and increase mobility.

# Cranberry Parsnip Juice

Two parsnips
One cup of cranberries
Four medium sized carrots
Four large stalks of celery
One lemon, peeled


Parsnips are not commonly juiced, a fact that makes this recipe unique. If you've never tried a parsnip juice, give this one a try. There are lots of great reasons to enjoy parsnip juice as a regular part of your diet. Parsnips contain an exceptionally wide variety of various nutrients, vitamins, and minerals. Parsnips are high in folate, potassium, dietary fiber, and vitamin C.

# Back Nine

Two cups of cranberries
One cups of strawberries
Three medium sized apples, any variety
One lime, peeled
One lemon, peeled

Although this is still a healthy juice, it has a relatively high sugar content due to all the fruits. For this reason this juice can be a nice treat once in awhile, but not something you would want to consumer every day. That said, this juice still has some serious health benefits, such as it's detoxifying ability. Strawberries are high in potassium and promote detoxification. They also aid in regulation of the blood pressure.

# Riding High

Five large carrots
One English cucumber
Two medium sized Granny Smith apples
One cup of cranberries
One whole lemon, peeled
One thumb sized piece of ginger root
One clove of garlic

This juice is rich in pectin and as such is a great way to combat high cholesterol. Pectin is found in both apples and carrots and has been definitively linked to substantial reductions in "LDL" cholesterol, aka "bad" cholesterol. There is also some evidence that ginger and lemon assist with the reduction of elevated cholesterol levels as well. The vitamin C in this juice which comes primarily from the carrots can also help to repair dry skin leaving you with skin that feels healthy and looks youthful.

# Cool Cucumber Cranberry Water

One large cucumber
Three stalks of celery
Three medium sized Red Delicious apples
One fennel bulb and stem
Half a cup of cranberries
One lime, peeled

A great juice to use as part of a juice cleanse due to its high water content from the cucumbers. It is also packed full of vitamins, in particular vitamin A and vitamin K, as well as a solid amount of potassium.

# Cayenne Cranberry Cracker

One large orange
Two large peaches
Two cups of chopped pineapple
One cup of cranberries
One lemon, peeled
One thumb sized piece of ginger
One pinch of cayenne pepper (stirred in after juicing)

This tasty juice provides all the vitamin C you need for a whole day. It is also a superb anti-cancer juice. The anti-oxidant power of the vitamin C works to rid the body of free radicals while the limioid compound in the oranges has been shown to fight a variety of different cancers including breast cancer, stomach cancer, colon cancer, and skin cancer.

# Quick and Easy Maintenance Juice

Two beetroot
Five medium sized carrots
One English cucumber
Three leaves of kale
One cup of broccoli florets
Two cloves of garlic

This juice is a great way to make sure you are getting your daily recommended amount of manganese and folate as beetroot is rich in both. This juice is simple and quick to prepare, with no frills, no fruit, and nothing sweet about it. It is a good juice for when you are in a rush or don't have many fruits or vegetables handy, but don't want to skimp on your vegetable consumption.

# Green, Rested, and Ready

One English cucumber
Two cups of spinach
Two handfuls of parsley
Two medium sized Granny Smith apples
Two leaves of kale
One stalk of celery
Three stalks of asparagus

This juice is as green as green can be. The apples provide a hint of sweetness that will make this drink a favorite even for people who dislike the taste of kale and spinach. The parsley in this juice will also help to reduce the gas and bloating that some people experience when juicing with raw kale. The spinach is a great intestinal tract cleanser that reduces the buildup of waste and facilitates the body's digestive system working efficiently without any digestive issues. The natural laxative found in apples also promotes regular bowel movements. This juice is also rich in vitamins and minerals that the body needs. For example, a small 15 oz glass of this juice provides an entire day's supply of vitamins C and K, as well as the mineral copper.

# Jumping Vegetable Juice

One cup of spinach
Two salad tomatoes
One handful of parsley
One medium sized red bell pepper
Six large stalks of celery
Six stalks of asparagus
Half a cup of cranberries
Half a lemon, peeled

This juice is focused on health and weight loss as it is very heavy on the vegetables as opposed to fruit. If you need an energy boost to get you through the day you can't go wrong with this juice as it is rich in both phosphorous and potassium. This juice is also a great recovery drink after a hard workout. This is due not only to the energy boost the juice delivers, but also due to its ability to reduce inflammation. Spinach is highly alkaline which can help to reduce inflammation. The tomatoes are also rich in inflammation-fighting vitamins and nutrients, many of which are contained in the skin of the tomato.

# Nature's Gift Juice

One medium sized green bell pepper
Four kiwi
Two cups of blackberries
One quarter pineapple
One thumb sized piece of ginger
Half a lemon, peeled

A smooth juice with just a hint of sour, this juice is always a hit
with those who love the taste of blackberries. Kiwi juice contains
high levels of antioxidants due to it's high levels of copper, iron,
and vitamins C and E. The antioxidant power of this juice
provides a boost to your immune system that can help the body to
prevent or quickly fight off colds or the flu.

# Time of Your Life Juice

Eight medium sized carrots
Two beetroot
Half a yam (sweet potato)
One medium sized green bell pepper
One Granny Smith apple

This juice is full of root vegetables that deliver a robust cleanse and reduces toxicity of the liver and improves conditions like hepatitis, food poisoning, diarrhea, vomiting, and jaundice. It is a great "reset" for your body after consuming alcohol as it cleanses the liver of the toxic alcohol it has been working to remove from your body. In addition to the cleansing power of beets, the carrots in this juice aid in the cleanse by functioning as a diuretic and forcing excess fluid out of the body.

Beets don't just cleanse the liver though, they also help to cleanse the blood, colon, and gall bladder. Within the bloodstream, the high iron content works to rebuild your red blood cell count so that your body can benefit from increased access to oxygen. In addition, the liver aids in the metabolization of fat. Keeping your liver cleansed and running efficiently promotes weight loss efficiency.

# Marathon Juice

Two large oranges
Two medium sized carrots
One large stalk of celery
One medium sized green bell pepper
One thumbnail sized piece of turmeric
One thumbnail sized piece of ginger
One lemon, peeled
Five leaves of peppermint

Studies have widely recognized turmeric to be a powerful anti-inflammatory agent. This is because turmeric contains at least six components that have anti-inflammatory effects. Further, more recent studies indicate strong evidence that turmeric also has anti-cancer properties. Despite this, our typical diets don't contain nearly enough turmeric! Juicing with turmeric is a convenient and delicious way to make sure you avail yourself of its many health benefits.

# Peaches Get Beaches

Six medium sized peaches
One medium sized red bell pepper
One half of a medium sized coconut (scoop the meat out and
discard the shell)
Half a large orange

This tasty tropical juice boasts big quantities of copper, iron,
potassium, phosphorus, magnesium, zinc, and selenium.

Selenium contributes to the proper function of the immune system
as well as the reproductive system. Magnesium promotes a
healthy bone density and together with zinc helps the body to
process the macronutrients we consume and turn them into energy
the body can use.

The minerals in this juice are important for a variety of important
functions within the body. Copper and iron work together to
improve the flow of oxygen through the bloodstream by boosting
the production of red and white blood cells.

# Superhero's Secret

Three medium sized guava
One medium sized green bell pepper
One medium clementine, peeled
One medium sized apple, any variety
One lime, peeled

Guava is not a popular fruit in many Western countries, which is really unfortunate for us! Guava is a delicious "super fruit" widely consumed in some tropical countries. It earned its reputation as a super fruit due to its high concentration of a wide variety of nutrients and its many health benefits. Among other vitamins, minerals, and nutrients, Guava is particularly rich in copper, vitamin C, lycopene, and antioxidants. If you aren't able to find guava at your local chain grocery store then try a smaller produce market, especially one that carries a variety of ethnic foods.

# Growing Big Juice

One medium sized stalk of broccoli
One medium sized cucumber
Three large carrots
Two handfuls of parsley
Four stalks of celery
Four stalks of asparagus
Two medium sized green bell pepper
Two table spoons of extra virgin olive oil (stir in after juicing)

This juice is an easy way to load up on folic acid and histamines which promote blood flow and improve circulation. This juice will give you an energetic feeling all over and beats slamming down another caffeine-laden energy drink or coffee when you're pulling an all-nighter.

# Rainbow Love Juice

One medium sized red bell pepper
Three medium sized carrots
Two large peeled oranges
Two beetroot
One medium sized apple
One medium sized pear
One lemon, peeled
Half a lime, unpeeled

Drinking this juice daily will could lower your risk of a heart attack by up to two thirds! That is because moderate, consistent carrot consumption has been shown in studies to reduce cholesterol level by about 10 percent. High cholesterol is a leading cause of heart disease, therefore carrot consumption promotes heart health by reducing your risk of heart disease. Consuming carrots regularly also reduces your risk of a heart attack. In fact, some studies show a dramatic decrease in heart attack risk when carrot consumption is maintained over the course of a year.

# Farm to Table Juice

Seven organic cherry tomatoes
Four stalks of asparagus
Two cups of spinach
Two medium sized green apples
Two medium sized carrots
Ten red grapes
Two large celery stalks

The high levels of potassium and magnesium in this juice, as well as the two cups of spinach, work together to lower elevated blood pressure. The juice from the green bell pepper contains powerful antioxidants that contribute to a reduction in cholesterol. This is a great juice for boosting your immune system, lowering your blood pressure, and losing weight.

# Crazy About Cruciferous

Eight leaves of kale
Fist-sized crown of broccoli
One English cucumber
One medium sized apples
One medium sized pear
One medium sized green bell pepper
Two cups of spinach
One lemon

A delicious, Kale based juice that is excellent for weight loss!
Kale is considered a "super food" and is ideal for weight loss due
to its high concentration of nutrients and low calorie content. It is
among the most nutrient-dense vegetables available and this juice
makes sure you can easily consume this amazing vegetable daily.
Kale is also a significant source of organo-sulfur compounds.
Studies show these compounds are effective at fighting many
different types of cancer. One of the many amazing qualities of
kale is that it can actually contribute to a destruction of cancer
cells within the body.

In addition to fighting cancer that already exists in the body, kale
has also been shown to prevent cancer from occurring in the first
place. The sulforaphane contents of kale has been shown to
reduce the risk of cancer from occurring in the body.

This drink also contains spinach, which is another vegetable
studies have shown to be effective in fighting and preventing
various types of cancer. The powerful anti-oxidants contained in
this vegetable contribute to the deceleration of cancerous cell
production and division.

# Pepper and Cabbage Juice

One quarter of a small head of green cabbage
One medium sized green bell pepper
One medium sized red bell pepper
Two medium sized Granny Smith apples
One cup of spinach
One thumb sized piece of ginger root
Two medium sized carrots
One stalk of celery
Half a lemon, peeled

This juice is super healthy, great for weight loss, and also helps sooth any digestive issues you may be experiencing. The natural laxative in apples can aid with constipation and promote regular bowel movements. The carrots work to cleanse the liver while stimulating a release of bile that is a key component of proper digestions. Juicing with lemon and ginger root not only adds a kick to the juice's flavor, but they also both aid in digestion by reducing gas buildup. Finally, the spinach works to cleanse the intestinal tract while promoting proper digestion.

# Lime in the Sky

Three large celery stalks
Four clementines, peeled
One apple, any red variety
One medium sized green bell pepper
One lemon, peeled
Two limes, peeled
Two cups of mint leaves

This is a great juice to have before a busy day where you'll be
burning up energy as it has just enough sugar in the oranges to get
you energized, but not so much that you'll endure a sudden post-
sugar crash. The generous helping of mint adds a unique kick to
the flavor of this juice that compliments the other fruits and
vegetables very well. Mint also delivers some surprising health
benefits. Mint has antimicrobial properties and has also been
shown to sooth a queasy stomach.

# Tingle Mingle

Three medium sized carrots
Half an English cucumber
One cup of strawberries
One cup of blueberries
One medium sized apple
One medium sized green bell pepper
Three cloves of garlic

This juice provides a powerful boost to the immune system. The carrots boost the production and efficiency of the white blood cells, which help to defend the body against a variety of infections. The high vitamin C content of the strawberries aid the body in fighting and preventing colds and the flu.

# Peppermint Pepper Juice

One medium sized orange
Five medium sized carrots
Three medium sized apples
Two large peaches
Half a lemon, peeled
One lime, peeled
One medium sized red bell pepper
Six leaves of peppermint

This juice is smooth and tasty and packs enough carrots to meaningfully reduce your "bad" LDL cholesterol levels by about 10 percent over time. High cholesterol is a leading cause of heart disease, therefore carrot consumption promotes heart health by reducing your risk of heart disease and also reducing your risk of a heart attack. This juice can radically improve your heart health while still tasting great.

# Millennium Apple Juice

Three large stalks of celery
Three medium sized apples
One medium sized green bell pepper
One large orange, peeled
One thumbnail sized piece of ginger root
One lemon, unpeeled
One lime, unpeeled
Two cloves of garlic

Think of this juice is a bit of a radical (but healthier!) twist on traditional apple juice. The celery is high in vitamins and minerals that help to maintain the skin's youthful elasticity and aid complexion. Celery can also help to calm the nerves and reduce high blood pressure. The orange juice also helps to protect the skin by attacking and eliminating free radicals within the body. This juice isn't for everyone but give it a try and see if you're one of the people who love it.

# The Mighty Toxin Slayer

Two  medium sized green bell pepper
Two medium sized green apples
One medium sized cucumber
One large stalk of celery
One cup of parsley
One cup of spinach
One lime, peeled

This juice is great for cleansing the body of toxins and facilitating enhanced liver and kidney function. The significant quantity of parsley also makes this juice a powerful immune system booster. Parsley is nutrient dense and provides a significant source of numerous vitamins including vitamin A, vitamin B 12, vitamin C, and vitamin K. Parsley has been shown to promote a strong immune system that keeps the whole body healthy and wards of colds, the flu, and other common ailments.

# Citrus in the Sun

One medium sized Granny Smith apple
One medium sized pear, any variety you like
Three stalks of celery
Half an English cucumber
One lemon, peeled
One medium sized green bell pepper
Two cups of spinach
Two leaves of kale

This is a great juice for improving your complexion and making you feel and look vibrant and youthful. The juice from the lemon functions as a natural antiseptic that promotes skin health. The sodium in the celery is jam-packed with minerals and vitamins which promote elasticity and youthful tightness in the skin. Between the apples and the kale, you're also consuming significant quantities of vitamins A, C, E, and K, all of which prevent the appearance of premature aging by reducing free radicals in the body.

This juice has a bold flavor that is all its own, with the sour lemon and sweet apple packing the most punch. Even if you are not a fan of the taste of kale, you will probably still like this juice as the taste is masked by the other ingredients.

# Mango Down

One medium sized red bell pepper
One large mango, peeled
Three clementines. Peeled
Ten green grapes
One lemon, peeled
One pear, any variety

This juice will wake you up and get you moving with it's fresh
mango flavor. It also gives you a substantial dose of vitamins A,
B, C, E, K, folate, niacin, riboflavin, calcium, and iron. A great
way to start your day!

# Redneck Relief

One English cucumber
Five strawberries
One medium sized green bell pepper
One cup of blueberries
Two leaves of kale
One third of a watermelon, rind removed
One lime, peeled
Half a lemon, peeled

This juice is sweet and has many health benefits, such as being rich in antioxidants due to the strawberries and blueberries. Despite the health benefits, it is a little heavy on the sugar content, so it is not the best juice for weight loss.

# Rough and Ready Juice

Five large carrots
Half a medium sized pineapple
One medium sized red bell pepper
Three large stalks of celery
Three strawberries
One lemon, peeled
One glove of garlic

The carrots in this juice promote a healthy cleanse by functioning as a diuretic and forcing excess fluid out of the body. In addition, the pineapple is rich in vitamins B6 and C, folate, beta carotene, and thiamin. This juice is a great way to ensure you get the recommended daily dose of potassium, magnesium, and copper. The pineapple and carrots also promote good heart health and can reduce the risk of heart disease while the strawberries add to its smooth and sweet taste.

# CNS Soother Juice

Three large carrots
One beetroot
One cup of spinach
One teaspoon of dried spirulina
One medium sized green bell pepper
Two large stalks of celery
One medium sized cucumber

This juice let's you bounce back and after a beating – a great juice after overindulging in alcohol! The beets in this juice works to reduce alcohol toxicity in the liver and promotes recovery by cleansing the blood and aiding in the delivering of oxygen via the bloodstream. The spinach also has cleansing properties and aids the restoration of the body's circulatory system. It has also been shown to promote brain health, which can help you recover from the mental fog a hang over faster. Finally, the calcium and magnesium in the celery stalks have been shown to ease agitation of the central nervous system.

# Happy Return Juice

One beetroot
One medium sized apple
Two medium sized carrots
One medium sized green bell pepper
Two cups of spinach
One cup of parsley
One large celery stalk
One cup of raspberries
Two thumb sized pieces of ginger

This juice offers a great internal cleanse. The beet juice reduces toxicity in the liver which can deliver fast relief from accidental food poisoning, diarrhea, and vomiting. It is also an excellent cure for a hangover due to the liver cleansing beetroot in the juice.

In addition to the beetroot, the apple (or apples) you use in this juice contain a natural laxative. Apple juice facilitates regular bowel movements which add to the cleansing power of this juice.

# Fast Fuel Up

One medium sized red bell pepper
One medium sized yam (sweet potato)
Three clementines, peeled
One beetroot
Two large carrots
Three medium sized apples
One thumb-sized piece of ginger

The beetroot in this juice is a great source of fast energy as your body can quickly digest the carbohydrates in the beetroot and use them to fuel your body throughout the day. This juice also facilitates proper digestion within the body and can aid indigestion. This is due to the natural laxative properties of apples. The juice in the apple promotes regular bowel movements. Carrots and beets also promote regular bowel movements by cleansing the liver and stimulating additional bile release which can aid constipation.

# Juicing is Believing

One beetroot
Four stalks of asparagus
Two large stalks of celery
Six medium sized carrots
Thumb sized portion of ginger
Half a peeled lemon
One cup of spinach
One medium sized Red Delicious apple

A solid choice for cleansing and detoxing. The root vegetables in this juice detoxify the liver, strengthen the blood, and aid with the reduction of any condition related to toxicity in the body, such as hepatitis, food poisoning, jaundice, and a hang over. While cleansing the body, this juice also provides an immediate energy boost that can last for hours.

# The Juicy Cruiser

One peeled mango
One quarter of a medium sized cantaloupe
One medium sized yellow bell pepper
Seven leaves of peppermint
One thumb sized piece of ginger
Half a medium sized cucumber

This is a great tasting juice that is best enjoyed in moderation due to the sugar content and the relative lack of health benefits compared to most of the other juices in this book. Despite the fact that it cracks the bottom 10% of juices in this book in terms of health benefits, it is still a much healthier choice than virtually any commercially available juice you could buy at the grocery store. It also manages to contain high levels of potassium as well as vitamins A and C. This can make it a good choice for warding off a cold or flu, as well as maintaining or improving the health of your skin, eyes, and immune system.

# Papaya Pepper Juice

One papaya
One medium sized green bell pepper
One medium sized orange bell pepper
One medium sized peach
Two medium sized clementines, peeled
Thumbnail sized piece of ginger
One lemon, peeled

This is a tasty and exotic juice that makes for a good source of vitamins A and C. It also contains plenty of antioxidants and potassium.

# Asparagus Turmeric Juice

Six medium sized carrots
Five stalks of asparagus
One English cucumber
Two medium sized pears, any variety
One large celery stalk
Five thumb sized pieces or turmeric
One thumbnail sized piece of ginger
Half a lemon, peeled

This juice is an impressive cold, flu, and fever remedy that works quickly to boost the body's immune system and fight off illness. If you are suffering from a fever in particular, consider doubling the quantity of ginger you are juicing. The lemon content in this juice facilitates perspiration while reducing feelings of nausea or dizziness. This juice also contains pears which are great for preventing a cold or flu or fighting one off by fortifying the body's immune system.

# The Born Juicer

Two cups of spinach
One leaf of kale
One medium sized green bell pepper
Two medium sized stalks of celery
Two medium sized apples, any variety
One large orange
One lemon, peeled
One lime, peeled
Three thumbnail sized pieces of ginger
Four cloves of garlic
Pinch of cayenne pepper (add after juicing)

This juice is a powerful cleaner and aids the functioning of the digestive system. Ginger has been shown to ease digestive issues such as nausea, dizziness, motion sickness, vomiting, or an upset stomach. In fact, studies have shown that ginger is actually superior to popular prescription medication when it comes to providing relief for digestive problems!

# Sun Up Juice Down

Six medium sized carrots
Two large oranges, peeled
One medium sized yellow bell pepper
One medium sized clementine, peeled
One lime, peeled
One dash of cayenne pepper (stirred in after juicing)

This carrot heavy juice is a great way to get your daily vitamins A and C requirement as well as loading up on beta-carotene. If you're bored of traditional orange juice, try a glass of this with your breakfast and break out of your breakfast boredom.

# Gut Be Gone Juice

Five leaves of kale
One cup of collard greens
One medium sized red bell pepper
One medium sized apple (any variety you like)
One medium sized green bell pepper
Two handfuls of cilantro
Two medium sized carrots
One medium sized cucumber
Fifteen red grapes

This juice is great for weight loss. The kale leaves and collard greens are extremely nutrient-dense, meaning they add very few calories to this juice while still managing to deliver a significant quantity of nutrients and anti-oxidants.

In addition to promoting overall bodily health and weight loss, this juice can be an effective cancer deterrent. The collard greens are rich in nutrients that have powerful cancer fighting properties. Studies have shown both kale and collard greens can be beneficial at fighting and preventing breast cancer, prostate cancer, colon cancer, and other cancers.

# Ultra Low Calorie Super Juice

Three cups of broccoli florets
Four leaves of kale
One medium sized green bell pepper
One English cucumber
Two stalks of celery
One lemon, peeled
One lime, peeled

This juice is rich in vitamins B, C, and K, as well as several important minerals. Broccoli and kale are both "nutrient dense" meaning that they are very low in calories while still being high in a variety of nutrients. Juicing with broccoli and kale has been shown to help prevent the deterioration of eye sight due to age-related conditions like macular degeneration.

Broccoli is also a powerful cleanser and detoxifier. Some of the nutrients contained in broccoli (such as glucoraphanin, gluconasturtiin, and glucobrassicin) facilitate a natural detoxification process in the body by working to activate, neutralize, and eliminate a variety of harmful contaminants.

# The Bitter Mint

One large pink grapefruit
One large orange, peeled
One medium sized red bell pepper
Four leaves of peppermint
Two cloves of garlic
One lime, peeled

An excellent weight loss juice and a fine way to get the day
started right with a high dose of vitamin C and antioxidants to
energize and strengthen the immune system. This juice is also
surprisingly filling due to the grapefruit content, which makes it a
great choice for a juice fast or weight loss regimen.

# Clued In Juice

Three Red Delicious apples
One large celery stalk
One medium sized cucumber
One medium sized green bell pepper
One cup of mint leaves
One cup of spinach
One lime, peeled
Half a lemon, peeled

Studies have shown that consuming the juices from apples and lemons can reduce breathing difficulties, improve oxygen intake, and even prevent the development of asthma in children. The pectin found in the apples has been definitively linked to substantial reductions in "LDL" cholesterol, aka "bad" cholesterol. There is also some evidence that lemon assists with the reduction of elevated cholesterol levels as well. The vitamin C in the apples can also help to repair dry skin leaving you with skin that feels healthy and looks youthful.

# Day by Day Juice

One third of a medium sized pineapple
Five green grapes
Two strawberries
Two large stalks of celery
One medium sized cucumber
One medium sized green bell pepper
One cup of mint leaves
Half a cup of spinach
Half a lemon, peeled
One thumb sized piece of ginger

This juice promotes good heart health and can reduce muscle inflammation, making it an ideal post-workout juice. This juice has a minty flavor that combines with the ginger for an interesting kick that is sure to delight the taste buds! But this juice isn't just a great tasting, refreshing treat. The heaping amount of pineapple is dense in myriad nutrients your body needs, including vitamins B6 and C, folate, beta carotene, and thiamin. It also contains high levels of minerals like potassium, magnesium, and copper.

# The Tight and Right Slim Down

One ruby red large grapefruit
Four medium sized carrots
One medium sized green bell pepper
Two large stalks of celery
One thumbnail sized piece of ginger
One medium sized lemon, peeled
Half an English cucumber

Ready to burn some fat? Grapefruit is great for weight loss and maintaining a healthy heart. Studies have shown that grapefruit consumption lowers the risk of diabetes by controlling insulin production and maintaining consistent blood sugar levels, which also helps to combat obesity. The high concentration of choline, potassium, lycopene, and vitamin C in grapefruit all promote heart health and have been shown to reduce the risk of heart disease.

# Out on Kale

Four stalks of celery
Six kale leaves
Three stalks of asparagus
Three apples, any variety
Three cloves of garlic
One lime, peeled
Half of one lemon, peeled

This juice is nutrient-dense due to all the kale leaves, making it an excellent weight loss juice. The garlic in the juice isn't for everyone, but those who like it tend to like it a lot! Garlic is highly nutritious, containing lots of maganese, fiber, selenium, calcium, copper, iron, and vitamins B1, B6, and C. Studies have shown garlic consumption can help prevent and cure the common cold. Garlic also works to lower cholesterol and blood pressure, and may aid with the prevention of certain brain diseases like Alzheimer's disease and dementia. This is probably due at least in part to the high antioxidant concentration.

# Pomegranate Pepper

One large pomegranate
One medium sized orange bell pepper
Two Red Delicious apples
One medium sized pear, any variety
Two clementines, peeled
One half of a lemon, peeled
Thumb sized piece of ginger root

Pomegranates are great sources of nutrients and anti-oxidants. Even by the standards of super foods known for their high anti-oxidant concentration, pomegranate gets top marks. There is very little fat in a pomegranate and no cholesterol at all. Pomegranate also contains lots of vitamin B5 that helps the body metabolize the macronutrients you consume, which makes this a great juice for anyone trying to lose some weight.

# Berry Asparagus Juice

Half a cup of raspberries
Half a cup of blueberries
One cup of strawberries
Three stalks of asparagus
One medium sized pear, any variety
One large pomegranate
Two medium sized clementines, peeled


This juice is another tasty anti-oxidant powerhouse with a bit
more sugar content due to the berries which means this is not such
a great weight loss juice. It is however a great source of iron,
calcium, zinc, magnesium and phosphorus.

# Be C-ing You

Three cups of strawberries
Two cups of blueberries
Two stalks of asparagus
One cup of mint
Three large apples, any variety
One English cucumber
One lime, peeled

This refreshing juice packs a full day's supply of vitamin C. It also has detoxifying power due to the high potassium content of the strawberries which also helps to regulate blood pressure. In addition to these benefits, strawberries are great for your mental health. Studies have shown that the folic acid found in strawberries facilitates enhanced cognition, memory, and focus. For this reason, this juice would be a perfect choice for studying or working on something that requires prolonged mental focus. Make enough to share it with a friend who doesn't normally juice, almost everyone loves this recipe!

# The Odd Couple

Four large leaves of red cabbage
One beetroot
Two large stalk of celery
One English cucumber
One medium sized red bell pepper
Three medium sized carrots
One quarter of a pineapple
Two handfuls of spinach
Half a lemon, peeled

The pineapple flavor in this juice helps to even out the earthiness of the beetroot. If it taste too much of beet or cabbage, you can always add some extra pineapple. However you juice it though, this recipe is extremely healthy as it is jam-packed with the vitamins and minerals your body needs.

This juice is a powerful cleanser. The beet juice aids in reducing liver toxicity and combats conditions relating to bile, such as food poisoning, jaundice, hepatitis, diarrhea, and vomiting. The spinach also aids in cleansing the body, especially the intestinal tract, while its high levels of iron help to fortify the blood.

# Greener and Cleaner

Five leaves of kale
Two large stalks of celery
Three medium sized Granny Smith apples
One medium sized green bell pepper
One medium sized cucumber
Two handfuls of spinach

A super green, tasty, healthy recipe. This juice is a solid choice for anyone wanting to focus on cleansing the body of toxins. Cleansing can be an effective way to jump start a recovery after a binge on unhealthy food or toxic substances like alcohol. It can also be a great way to energize the body even when you normally eat well and live an active lifestyle. If you are doing a juice cleanse, make this drink a staple of the cleanse by drinking it either daily or every other day.

# Grape Expectations

One honeydew melon, chopped
One Bartlett pear
Two medium sized Red Delicious apples
Two stalks of asparagus
Five red grapes
Five green grapes
One lime, peeled

Lots of folks love the taste of honeydew melon, but just don't
make an effort to consume it regularily. Not only do honeydew
melons taste great and yield lots of juice, but they are also a great
source of carotenoids. Carotenoids has been shown to promote a
variety of desirable health benefits including decreasing the risk
of particular cancers and eye diseases. They also have protective
benefits for the skin that will help you look and feel younger.
Reproductive health and bone density can also improve with
regular consumption of carotenoids. The grapes in this juice add a
nice, complementary flavor to the melon and more than that, they
also contain a variety of anti-inflammatory nutrients that promote
longevity!

# Grounded and Happy

Three medium sized apples, any variety
Two beetroot
Seven large carrots
One medium sized green bell pepper
One quarter of a medium sized pineapple
One thumb sized piece of garlic

An earthy but very drinkable cleansing juice! Beetroot is rich in key minerals like potassium, magnesium, and iron. It also packs in high levels of vitamins A, B6 and C. In addition, it is rich in anti-oxidants and low in calories. The apple and the pineapple provide enough of a sweet flavor that the taste of beet is toned down greatly in this juice.

# Dancing the Juicer Jig

Two cups of fresh chopped coconut
Three medium sized carrots
Two Granny Smith apples
One medium sized green bell pepper
One medium sized clementine
One clove of garlic
One thumb sized ginger

A great juice to reinvigorate yourself after a long day at work. This is a great tasting juice with a noticeable sweetness that isn't overpowering. The texture is smooth and creamy, and the "zing" can be amped up by doubling the ginger content. The color is a rich and creamy orange and it provides the delicious and refreshing flavor of coconut while also containing significant nutrients and anti-oxidants that will energize the body for hours.

# Cruciferous Calorie Burner

Five leaves of kale
Five leaves of box choy
One cup of spinach
One cup of broccoli florets
Three large stalks of celery
Two stalks of asparagus
One English cucumber
One lemon, peeled

Juicing with cruciferous vegetables means that you can easily get an entire day's supply of many vitamins and nutrients while hardly consuming any calories. Kale is such a healthy vegetable that you'll want to consume it as often as possible. You can cycle through the various kale recipes in this book to keep yourself from getting bored. Juices with significant kale quantity and little to no fruit, like this juice, are excellent juices for weight loss. This is because kale is extremely nutrient dense.

# Pride of California

Two beetroot
Four leaves of kale
Three leaves of Romaine lettuce
One medium sized green bell pepper
One English cucumber
Two large stalks of celery
Four large sized carrots
One medium sized clementine, peeled

A delicious "almost green" juice with some carrot, clementine, and beet thrown in. That means that in addition to all of the health benefits of a green juice, you also get the powerful cleansing ability of beet that aids the body in purging toxins and enhancing the health of organs like the kidney and liver.

# Summer's Bone

Two medium sized pears
Two leaves of kale
One medium sized red bell pepper
One medium sized yam (sweet potato)
One large orange, peeled
Three large stalks of celery
One lime, peeled

A great juice for promoting all-around health benefits. This juice not only tastes great, it also has some impressive health benefits as well as it is high in folate, niacin, riboflavin, and vitamins B-6 and K. The pears are also high in boron which prevents calcium loss and promotes bone health. The pears also contain high levels of anti-oxidants and can fight high blood pressure as well as reduce inflammation.

# Sky High Spice

Four large stalks of celery
One medium sized orange bell pepper
One large slice of pineapple (chop if needed)
One medium sized apple (any variety you like)
One lemon, peeled
One thumbnail sized piece of ginger
One table spoon of cayenne pepper (stir in after juicing)

A sweet tasting juice that is still healthy! This juice is consistently a favorite for its great taste, but it can also improve your the function of your cardiovascular system. Studies have shown that consuming the juices from apples and lemons can reduce breathing difficulties, improve oxygen intake, and even prevent the development of asthma in children. The ginger in this juice will also aid in reduction of inflammation which can reduce pain and increase mobility.

# Fresh Parsnip Change Up

Two parsnips
Four medium sized carrots
One medium sized red bell pepper
Two large stalks of celery
One lemon, peeled
One lime, peeled
Half a table spoon of pumpkin pie spice (add after juicing)

An unconventional recipe that is healthy and tasty! There are lots of great reasons to enjoy parsnip juice as a regular part of your diet. Parsnips contain an exceptionally wide variety of various nutrients, vitamins, and minerals. Parsnips are high in folate, potassium, dietary fiber, and vitamin C.

# The Night Capper

Three cups of strawberries
Three medium sized apples, any variety
One medium sized cucumber
One medium sized green bell pepper
Two thumb-sized pieces of ginger

Although this is still a healthy juice, it has a relatively high sugar content due to all the fruit and berry content. For this reason this juice can be a nice treat once in awhile, but not something you would want to consumer every day. That said, this juice still has some serious health benefits, such as it's detoxifying ability. Strawberries are high in potassium and promote detoxification. They also aid in regulation of the blood pressure.

# The Pectin Solution

Five large carrots
One medium sized Granny Smith apple
One English cucumber
One medium sized yellow bell pepper
One medium sized orange, peeled
One lemon, peeled
One thumb sized piece of ginger root
One clove of garlic

This juice is rich in pectin and as such is a great way to combat high cholesterol. Pectin is found in both apples and carrots and has been definitively linked to substantial reductions in "LDL" cholesterol, aka "bad" cholesterol. There is also some evidence that ginger and lemon assist with the reduction of elevated cholesterol levels as well. The vitamin C in this juice which comes primarily from the carrots can also help to repair dry skin leaving you with skin that feels healthy and looks youthful.

# The Summer Sprinkler

One large cucumber
Three stalks of celery
Three medium sized Red Delicious apples
One medium sized green bell pepper
One fennel bulb and stem
One cup of spinach
One lime, peeled

A great juice to use as part of a juice cleanse due to its high water content from the cucumbers. It is also packed full of vitamins, in particular vitamin A and vitamin K, as well as a solid amount of potassium. The spinach contributes to the cleansing power of this juice as it works its way through your intestinal tract.

# C Day

One large orange
Three large peaches
One cup of pineapple (chopped)
One medium sized pear, any variety
One medium sized red bell pepper
One lemon, peeled
One thumb sized piece of ginger
One pinch of cayenne pepper (stirred in after juicing)

This tasty juice provides all the vitamin C you need for a whole day. It is also a superb anti-cancer juice. The anti-oxidant power of the vitamin C works to rid the body of free radicals while the liminoid compound in the oranges has been shown to fight a variety of different cancers including breast cancer, stomach cancer, colon cancer, and skin cancer.

# Veggie Heavy

Two beetroot
Five medium sized carrots
Two stalks of celery
One English cucumber
Four stalks of asparagus
Two cloves of garlic

This juice is a great way to make sure you are getting your daily
recommended amount of manganese and folate as beetroot is rich
in both. This juice is simple and quick to prepare, with no frills,
no fruit, and nothing sweet about it. It is a good juice for when
you are in a rush or don't have many fruits or vegetables handy,
but don't want to skimp on your vegetable consumption.

# CK Lax

Five leaves of kale
Three handfuls of parsley
One English cucumber
One medium sized red bell pepper
Two stalks of celery
One cup of spinach
One medium sized Granny Smith apple

This juice is as green as green can be. The apple provides a hint of sweetness that will make this drink a favorite even for people who dislike the taste of kale and spinach. The parsley in this juice will also help to reduce the gas and bloating that some people experience when juicing with raw kale. The spinach is a great intestinal tract cleanser that reduces the buildup of waste and facilitates the body's digestive system working efficiently without any digestive issues. The natural laxative found in apples also promotes regular bowel movements. This juice is also rich in vitamins and minerals that the body needs. For example, a small 15 oz glass of this juice provides an entire day's supply of vitamins C and K, as well as the mineral copper.

# Alkaline Top Up

One cup of spinach
One salad tomato
Two handfuls of parsley
Five large stalks of celery
One medium sized green bell pepper
One medium sized red bell pepper
One lemon, peeled

This juice is focused on health and weight loss as it is very heavy on the vegetables as opposed to fruit. If you need an energy boost to get you through the day you can't go wrong with this juice as it is rich in both phosphorous and potassium.

Pair this juice with a hard workout to kick your weight loss into high gear. This juice will help you recover after tearing it up in the gym. This is due not only to the energy boost the juice delivers, but also due to its ability to reduce inflammation. Spinach is highly alkaline which can help to reduce inflammation. The tomatoes are also rich in inflammation-fighting vitamins and nutrients, many of which are contained in the skin of the tomato.

# Heart-y Sprouts and Carrots

Four Brussels sprouts
One beetroot
One medium sized apple
One medium sized tangerine
Five medium sized carrots
Half a lemon
Two large peeled oranges

Moderate, consistent carrot consumption has been shown in studies to reduce cholesterol level by about 10 percent. High cholesterol is a leading cause of heart disease, therefore carrot consumption promotes heart health by reducing your risk of heart disease. Consuming carrots regularly also reduces your risk of a heart attack. In fact, some studies show a dramatic decrease in heart attack risk when carrot consumption is maintained over the course of a year. Drinking this juice daily will could lower your risk of a heart attack by up to two thirds!

# Forever Young

One medium sized tangerine
One medium sized green bell pepper
One large cucumber
Two cups of spinach
Two medium sized green apples
Two Brussels sprouts
Three medium sized carrots
Twenty grapes, any variety you like
One medium sized tomato

This is a great juice for boosting your immune system, lowering your blood pressure, and losing weight. The high levels of potassium and magnesium in this juice, as well as the two cups of spinach, work together to lower elevated blood pressure. The juice from the green bell pepper contains powerful antioxidants that contribute to a reduction in cholesterol.

Some people find this drink isn't sweet enough for them. If you like it a little sweeter, simply double or even triple the number of grapes and use a slightly smaller cucumber instead.

# Super Chill and Cool

One medium sized tangerine
One large cucumber
Six Brussels sprouts
Six leaves of kale
Two medium sized apples
Two cups of spinach
One lemon

This is a new healthy spin on a classic refreshing summer favorite, lemonade. And best of all, instead of being loaded with refined sugar like most commercial lemonades available at the grocery store, this juice is great for weight loss while still quenching your thirst with a delicious taste. It contains a significant amount of raw kale. Kale is considered a "super food" and is ideal for weight loss due to its high concentration of nutrients and low calorie content. It is among the most nutrient-dense vegetables available and this juice makes sure you can easily consume this amazing vegetable daily. Kale is also a significant source of organo-sulfur compounds. Studies show these compounds are effective at fighting many different types of cancer. One of the many amazing qualities of kale is that it can actually contribute to a destruction of cancer cells within the body. In addition to fighting cancer that already exists in the body, kale has also been shown to prevent cancer from occurring in the first place. The sulforaphane contents of kale has been shown to reduce the risk of cancer from occurring in the body.

This juice also contains spinach, which is another vegetable studies have shown to be effective in fighting and preventing various types of cancer. The powerful anti-oxidants contained in this vegetable contribute to the deceleration of cancerous cell production and division.

# Spinach Sprout Special

One quarter of a small head of red cabbage
Four Brussels sprouts
Three medium sized red apples (Gala, Macintosh, etc.)
Two cloves of garlic
One cup of spinach
One medium sized tangerine
One thumb sized piece of ginger root
Five medium sized carrots
One lemon

If you're looking for a way to incorporate more cabbage into your diet but you aren't a big fan of the taste, this juice could be the answer you've been waiting for. This is also a great juice if you're looking to sooth any digestive issues you may be experiencing. The natural laxative in apples can aid with constipation and promote regular bowel movements. The carrots work to cleanse the liver while stimulating a release of bile that is a key component of proper digestions. Juicing with lemon and ginger root not only adds a kick to the juice's flavor, but they also both aid in digestion by reducing gas buildup. Finally, the spinach works to cleanse the intestinal tract while promoting proper digestion.

# In It To Mint It

One large orange
One medium sized tangerine
Two Brussels sprouts
Two apples, any variety
One cucumber
One lemon, peeled
Two cups of mint leaves

This is a great pre-workout beverage as it has just enough sugar in the oranges to get you energized, but not so much that you'll endure a sudden post-sugar crash. The generous helping of mint adds a unique kick to the flavor of this juice that compliments the other fruits and vegetables very well. Mint also delivers some surprising health benefits. Mint has antimicrobial properties and has also been shown to sooth a queasy stomach.

# Ready to Run

Eight medium sized carrots
Two Brussels sprouts
One and a half cups of strawberries
One medium sized apple
One medium sized tangerine
One quarter of a lemon, peeled

This is a filling juice that provides a delicious way to get all the benefits of carrots while masking their flavor with the sweet taste of strawberries. The combination of carrots and strawberries is a favorite flavor of many people who juice regularly. In terms of health benefits, this juice provides a powerful boost to the immune system. The carrots boost the production and efficiency of the white blood cells, which help to defend the body against a variety of infections. The high vitamin C content of the strawberries aid the body in fighting and preventing colds and the flu.

# Subtle Carrot Sprout Juice

Eight medium sized carrots (or six large carrots)
Six Brussels sprouts
Three medium sized apples
One medium sized tangerine
Two stalks of asparagus
One medium sized orange
Three large peaches
Half a lemon, peeled

Don't be fooled by all the carrots you're juicing, the end result of this recipe is a smooth, sweet, peachy drink perfect for relaxing outside on a nice summer day. Even if you dislike the taste of carrots, it is important to consume them regularly. Regular carrot consumption has been shown to reduce "bad" LDL cholesterol levels by about 10 percent. High cholesterol is a leading cause of heart disease, therefore carrot consumption promotes heart health by reducing your risk of heart disease and also reducing your risk of a heart attack. This juice can radically improve your heart health while still tasting like a dream.

# Easy Living Tangerine Juice

Four medium sized tangerines
One medium sized apple, any variety
Five Brussels sprouts
Three large stalks of celery
One large orange, peeled
One thumbnail sized piece of ginger root

Think of this juice as a new healthier twist on traditional apple juice. The celery, although perhaps not the tastiest produce, is high in vitamins and minerals that help to maintain the skin's youthful elasticity and aid complexion. Celery can also help to calm the nerves and reduce high blood pressure. The orange juice also helps to protect the skin by attacking and eliminating free radicals within the body.

# Quiet Power Up

Two medium sized green apples (i.e. Granny Smith)
One medium sized cucumber
One medium sized tangerine
Two cups of parsley
One cup of spinach
Two Brussels sprouts
One half of a lime, peeled

This juice is great for cleansing the body of toxins and facilitating
enhanced liver and kidney function. The significant quantity of
parsley also makes this juice a powerful immune system booster.
Parsley has been shown to promote a strong immune system that
keeps the whole body healthy and wards of colds, the flu, and
other common ailments. Parsley is nutrient dense and provides a
significant source of numerous vitamins including vitamin A,
vitamin B 12, vitamin C, and vitamin K.

# Citrus Living

Four stalks of celery
Six Brussels sprouts
One medium sized tangerine
One peeled lemon
Three medium sized Granny Smith apples (granny smith)
One medium sized pear, any variety you like
Four cups of spinach
Three leaves of kale


This juice has a bold flavor that is all its own, with the sour lemon and sweet apple packing the most punch. Even if you are not a fan of the taste of kale, you will probably still like this juice as the taste is masked by the other ingredients. This is a great juice for improving your complexion and making you feel and look vibrant and youthful. The juice from the lemon functions as a natural antiseptic that promotes skin health. The sodium in the celery is jam-packed with minerals and vitamins which promote elasticity and youthful tightness in the skin. Between the apples and the kale, you're also consuming significant quantities of vitamins A, C, E, and K, all of which prevent the appearance of premature aging by reducing free radicals in the body.

# The Jogger's Daily Juice

One large mango, peeled (or two smaller sized mangos)
One medium sized tangerine
One large orange, peeled
Four Brussels sprouts
Half a lemon, unpeeled
Two medium sized apples
Cayenne pepper (to taste, start with one pinch)

This juice will wake you up and get you moving with it's fresh mango flavor and cayenne pepper kick! It also gives you a substantial dose of vitamins A, B, C, E, K, folate, niacin, riboflavin, calcium, and iron. A great way to start your day!

# Delight in Desert

One third of a watermelon, rind removed
One third of a pineapple, rind removed
Two Brussels sprouts
Six strawberries
One cup of blueberries
One medium sized tangerine
Half a lime, peeled

This juice is consistently a favorite for it's sweet, delicious taste. Unfortunately this sweet taste comes with a relatively high amount of sugar, meaning this juice really is more of a "treat" than something you would want to enjoy daily. Despite the sugar, the juice still has many health benefits, such as being rich in antioxidants due to the strawberries and blueberries. This juice is a great way to treat yourself without feeling too guilty.

# Sipping On Summertime

Half a medium sized pineapple
Six Brussels sprouts
Three stalks of asparagus
One medium sized tangerine
Two large carrots
One large stalk of celery
Half of one lemon, peeled
One glove of garlic

Although it is named after summer, the sweet flavor of this juice means you'll love drinking it at any time of the day or year. And it is not just the taste that makes this juice a popular favorite. The carrots in this juice promote a healthy cleanse by functioning as a diuretic and forcing excess fluid out of the body. In addition, the pineapple is rich in vitamins B6 and C, folate, beta carotene, and thiamin. This juice is a great way to ensure you get the recommended daily dose of potassium, magnesium, and copper. The pineapples and carrots also promote good heart health and can reduce the risk of heart disease.

# Tangerine Dream

One and a half cups of blackberries
Three medium sized tangerine
Two kiwi
One quarter pineapple
One medium sized pear
Two Brussels sprouts
Five leaves of peppermint

A smooth juice with just a hint of sour, this juice is always a hit with those who love the taste of blackberries. Pear juice contains high levels of antioxidants, as does the kiwi juice due to it's high levels of copper, iron, and vitamins C and E. The anti-oxidant power of this juice provides a boost to your immune system that can help the body to prevent or quickly fight off colds or the flu.

# Veggie Ho!

Eight large carrots (or twelve medium carrots)
Five stalks of asparagus
One beetroot
One yam (sweet potato)
Three Brussels sprouts

This juice is full of root vegetables that deliver a robust cleanse with a creamy, earthy flavor. Beet juice greatly reduces toxicity of the liver and improves conditions like hepatitis, food poisoning, diarrhea, vomiting, and jaundice. It is a great "reset" for your body after consuming alcohol as it cleanses the liver of the toxic alcohol it has been working to remove from your body. In addition to the cleansing power of beets, the carrots in this juice aid in the cleanse by functioning as a diuretic and forcing excess fluid out of the body.

Beets don't just cleanse the liver though, they also help to cleanse the blood, colon, and gall bladder. Within the bloodstream, the high iron content works to rebuild your red blood cell count so that your body can benefit from increased access to oxygen. In addition, the liver aids in the metabolization of fat. Keeping your liver cleansed and running efficiently promotes weight loss efficiency.

# Swinging Hammock Juice

Three medium sized carrots
Two medium sized tangerines
Six Brussels sprouts
Three large stalks of celery
Two thumbnail sized piece of turmeric
One thumbnail sized piece of ginger
Half of one lemon, unpeeled

Studies have widely recognized curcumin, a component of turmeric, as a powerful anti-inflammatory agent. In fact, turmeric contains at least five other components that also have anti-inflammatory effects. Further, more recent studies indicate strong evidence that turmeric also has anti-cancer properties. Despite this, our typical diets don't contain nearly enough turmeric! Juicing with turmeric is a convenient and delicious way to make sure you avail yourself of its many health benefits.

# Fast and Simple Powerhouse

One medium sized coconut (scoop the meat out and discard the shell)
Three medium sized tangerines
Two Brussels sprouts
Four medium sized peaches

This tasty tropical juice boasts big quantities of copper, iron, potassium, phosphorus, magnesium, zinc, and selenium. These minerals are important for a variety of important functions within the body. Copper and iron work together to improve the flow of oxygen through the bloodstream by boosting the production of red and white blood cells. Selenium contributes to the proper function of the immune system as well as the reproductive system. Magnesium promotes a healthy bone density and together with zinc helps the body to process the macronutrients we consume and turn them into energy the body can use.

# Vitamin Concentration Connection

Two medium sized guava, or one large guava (peeled or unpeeled according to preference)
One ruby red grapefruit
One medium sized tangerine
One kiwi
Two Brussels sprouts
One medium sized apple, any variety

Guava is not a popular fruit in many Western countries, which is really unfortunate for us! Guava is a delicious "super fruit" widely consumed in some tropical countries. It earned its reputation as a super fruit due to its high concentration of a wide variety of nutrients and its many health benefits. Among other vitamins, minerals, and nutrients, Guava is particularly rich in copper, vitamin C, lycopene, and antioxidants. If you aren't able to find guava at your local chain grocery store then try a smaller produce market, especially one that carries a variety of ethnic foods.

# Farmer's Cocktail

Three large carrots
Six Brussels sprouts
Two medium sized Granny Smith apples
Two medium sized tangerine
One handful of parsley
Two stalks of celery
Five stalks of asparagus
One medium sized stalk of broccoli
One medium sized cucumber

Don't let the mild taste of this juice fool you, this recipe delivers a high powered boost to your libido in an otherwise subtle and unassuming juice. Studies have shown that a lack of histamines in the body can cause difficulty reaching orgasm and a lack of interest in sex. The juiced asparagus stalks are a great source of folic acid which promotes the production of libido-enhancing histamines. Parsley has also been shown to improve blood flow which can enhance sexual stimulation.

# Leaving Las Vegas

Two medium sized tangerines
One beetroot
Four Brussels sprouts
Three cups of spinach
One teaspoon of dried spirulina
Two large stalks of celery

This juice is a great choice after a weekend of indulging in alcohol. The beets in this juice works to reduce alcohol toxicity in the liver and promotes recovery by cleansing the blood and aiding in the delivering of oxygen via the bloodstream. The spinach also has cleansing properties and aids the restoration of the body's circulatory system. It has also been shown to promote brain health, which can help you recover from the mental fog a hang over faster. Finally, the calcium and magnesium in the celery stalks have been shown to ease agitation of the central nervous system.

# Taste of Home

One beetroot
Four stalks of asparagus
One medium sized tangerine
One medium sized apple
Ten medium sized carrots
Four cups of spinach
One large celery stalk
One cup of raspberries

If you don't like the taste of beets, this may not be the juice for you (although you could always sweeten it up with an extra apple if you want to). Like the other beetroot heavy juices in this book, this one is another great internal cleanse. The beet juice reduces toxicity in the liver which can deliver fast relief from accidental food poisoning, diarrhea, and vomiting. It is also an excellent cure for a hangover due to the liver cleansing beetroot in the juice.

In addition to the beetroot, the apple (or apples) you use in this juice contain a natural laxative. Apple juice facilitates regular bowel movements which add to the cleansing power of this juice.

# The Glow Worm

One beetroot
Two large stalks of celery
One medium sized tangerine
One large carrot
Two medium sized apples
One medium sized yam (sweet potato)
One large orange, peeled

This juice packs a sweet flavor in a vibrant pink liquid. The appearance is sure to impress friends with whom you'll want to share this healthy and delicious recipe. Like it's bright pink color, this juice will make you feel vibrant and energized. The beetroot is a great source of fast energy as your body can quickly digest the carbohydrates in the beetroot and use them to fuel your body throughout the day.

This juice also facilitates proper digestion within the body and can aid indigestion. This is due to the natural laxative properties of apples. The juice in the apple promotes regular bowel movements. Carrots and beets also promote regular bowel movements by cleansing the liver and stimulating additional bile release which can aid constipation.

# Vivid Resurrection

One beetroot
One Granny Smith apple
One large sized apple, or two smaller sized apples (any variety
you like)
One large stalk of celery
Five medium sized carrots
Thumbnail sized portion of ginger
Half a peeled lemon
One peeled lime

When it comes to cleansing, this juice is hard to "beet". The root
vegetables in this juice detoxify the liver, strengthen the blood,
and aid with the reduction of any condition related to toxicity in
the body, such as hepatitis, food poisoning, jaundice, and a hang
over. While cleansing the body, this juice also provides an
immediate energy boost that can last for hours. You can add more
lemon, ginger, or apples if you want to tweak the taste and reduce
the earthy beet flavor.

# Singapore Sunshine

Half a medium sized cantaloupe
One medium sized tangerine
Two peeled mangos
Ten leaves of peppermint

This is a great tasting juice that is best enjoyed in moderation due
to the sugar content and the relative lack of health benefits
compared to most of the other juices in this book. Despite its
status as more of a "dessert juice" it still manages to contain high
levels of potassium as well as vitamins A and C. This can make it
a good choice for warding off a cold or flu, as well as maintaining
or improving the health of your skin, eyes, and immune system.

# The Mover and Shaker Blend

Two papaya
One medium sized peach
One medium sized tangerine
One medium sized apple, any variety
Two stalks of asparagus
One clove of garlic
Thumbnail sized piece of ginger

This is a tasty and exotic juice that makes for a good source of vitamins A and C. It also contains plenty of antioxidants and potassium. Try swapping out your plain old morning orange juice for this and get your day started right.

# Fed Up with Fat

Eight thumb sized pieces or turmeric
Four Brussels sprouts
Three medium sized carrots
Three medium sized apples
Three large celery stalks
One medium sized pear
One medium sized tangerine
One thumbnail sized piece of ginger
Two peeled lemons

With all of the apples and pears, this juice is a little heavy on the sugar and as such it is not the best choice for a daily juice aimed at promoting weight loss. It is however a powerful cold, flu, and fever remedy that works quickly to boost the body's immune system and fight off illness. If you are suffering from a fever in particular, consider doubling the quantity of ginger you are juicing. The heavy lemon content in this juice facilitates perspiration while reducing feelings of nausea or dizziness. This juice also contains many pears which are great for preventing a cold or flu or fighting one off by fortifying the body's immune system.

# The Stomach Settler

One medium sized stalk of celery
One medium sized cucumber
One medium sized apple, any variety
One medium sized tangerine
Half of one lemon, peeled
Half of one lime, peeled
One cup of spinach
Two thumbnail sized pieces of ginger
One clove of garlic

Ginger isn't a flavor for everyone, but those who like it will definitely want to give this juice a try. Even those who do not like the taste of ginger may still appreciate this juice for it's effect on the digestive system. Ginger has been shown to ease digestive issues such as nausea, dizziness, motion sickness, vomiting, or an upset stomach. In fact, studies have shown that ginger is actually superior to popular prescription medication when it comes to providing relief for digestive problems!

# Option A Overkill

Ten medium sized carrots
One medium sized tangerine
One large cucumber
One handful of cilantro
One thumbnail sized piece of ginger root
Half a lemon
Half a lime
One dash of cayenne pepper (stirred in after juicing)

This carrot heavy juice is a great way to improve your eyesight
and prevent certain diseases that effect the eye. Studies have
shown that a deficiency in vitamin A can impair the ability to see
in dim light. This juice contains approximately 500% of the
required daily dose of vitamin A which makes it ideal for boosting
this crucial vitamin in those who may be deficient. The beta-
carotene in this juice is also an effective way to prevent macular
degeneration, a common condition that impairs sight as the body
ages. Studies have shown that people who consistently consume
large quantities of beta-carotene can cut their risk of macular
degeneration in half.

# Rain Breaker

Five leaves of kale
One medium sized tangerine
One cup of collard greens
One medium sized red bell pepper
One medium sized apple (any variety you like)
Two handfuls of cilantro
Four Brussels sprouts
Five medium sized carrots

In addition to promoting overall bodily health, this juice can be an effective cancer deterrent. The collard greens are rich in nutrients that have powerful cancer fighting properties. Studies have shown both kale and collard greens can be beneficial at fighting and preventing breast cancer, prostate cancer, colon cancer, and other cancers.

This juice is also a great juice for weight loss. The kale leaves and collard greens are extremely nutrient-dense, meaning they add very few calories to this juice while still managing to deliver a significant quantity of nutrients and anti-oxidants.

# Broccoli Sweetheart

One cup of broccoli florets
Four Brussels sprouts
One medium sized apple
Two medium sized tangerines
Half a lemon, peeled

Most of us don't eat enough broccoli, which is unfortunate because this vegetable contains high levels of vitamins B, C, and K, as well as several important minerals. Broccoli is "nutrient dense" meaning that it is very low in calories while still being high in a variety of nutrients. Juicing with broccoli has been shown to help prevent the deterioration of eye sight due to age-related conditions like macular degeneration.

Broccoli is also a powerful cleanser and detoxifier. Some of the nutrients contained in broccoli (such as glucoraphanin, gluconasturtiin, and glucobrassicin) facilitate a natural detoxification process in the body by working to activate, neutralize, and eliminate a variety of harmful contaminants.

# Jive and Jazz Juice

One large pink grapefruit
Three medium sized tangerines
Half a cup of mint
Two cloves of garlic

This is a simple juice recipe that is easy to whip up first thing in the morning to enjoy with breakfast. It's a great way to get the day started right with a high dose of vitamin C and antioxidants to energize and strengthen the immune system. This juice is also surprisingly filling due to the grapefruit content, which makes it a great choice for a juice fast or weight loss regimen.

# King of the Hill

Three Granny Smith apples
Four large celery stalks
Five stalks of asparagus
One and a half cups of mint leaves
One cup of spinach
One small lime (or half of one large lime), peeled
One half of a lemon, peeled

Studies have shown that consuming the juices from apples and lemons can reduce breathing difficulties, improve oxygen intake, and even prevent the development of asthma in children. The pectin found in the apples has been definitively linked to substantial reductions in "LDL" cholesterol, aka "bad" cholesterol. There is also some evidence that lemon assists with the reduction of elevated cholesterol levels as well. The vitamin C in the apples can also help to repair dry skin leaving you with skin that feels healthy and looks youthful.

# The After Show

One third of a medium sized pineapple
One large stalk of celery
One medium sized cucumber
One cup of mint leaves
Two medium sized tangerines
One cup of spinach
Half of one lemon, unpeeled

This is a refreshing juice inspired by the beautiful tropical weather and relaxed hospitality of the Dominican Republic. It's minty flavor is sure to delight the taste buds! But this juice isn't just a great tasting, refreshing treat. The heaping amount of pineapple is dense in myriad nutrients your body needs, including vitamins B6 and C, folate, beta carotene, and thiamin. It also contains high levels of minerals like potassium, magnesium, and copper. Studies have shown that regularly consuming pineapple promotes good heart health and can reduce muscle inflammation. For this reason, this juice is great to enjoy after some physical activity.

# Ripe and No Gripe

One large grapefruit (any variety you like)
Three medium sized tangerines
Three medium sized carrots
One thumbnail sized piece of ginger

Grapefruit is great for weight loss and maintaining a healthy
heart. Studies have shown that grapefruit consumption lowers the
risk of diabetes by controlling insulin production and maintaining
consistent blood sugar levels, which also helps to combat obesity.
The high concentration of choline, potassium, lycopene, and
vitamin C in grapefruit all promote heart health and have been
shown to reduce the risk of heart disease.

# The Blueberry Bell Ringer

One English cucumber
One cup of blueberries
Three medium sized carrots
One red apple (Macintosh, Pink Lady, or any other red variety you like)
Two thumb sized pieces of ginger
One cup of fresh chopped coconut (or substitute for coconut milk)

This is a great tasting juice with a noticeable sweetness that isn't overpowering. The texture is smooth and creamy, and the "zing" can be amped up by doubling the ginger content. The color is a rich and creamy orange and it provides the delicious and refreshing flavor of coconut while also containing significant nutrients and anti-oxidants that will energize the body for hours. A great juice to reinvigorate yourself after a long day at work.

# Getting Cruciferous With It

Four Brussels sprouts
Four leaves of kale
Two large stalks of celery
One small cucumber (or half of one medium sized cucumber)
One medium sized tangerine
One lime, peeled
One cup of spinach
One cup of broccoli florets

Kale is such a healthy vegetable that you'll want to consume it as often as possible. You can cycle through the various kale recipes in this book to keep yourself from getting bored. Juices with significant kale quantity and little to no fruit, like this juice, are excellent juices for weight loss. This is because kale is extremely nutrient dense. Drinking kale juice means that you can easily get an entire day's supply of many vitamins and nutrients while hardly consuming any calories.

# Half Head Humdinger

One beetroot
One medium sized cucumber
Three large stalks of celery
Four large sized carrots
One cup of chopped coconut
Three leaves of kale
Half a head of romaine lettuce

In addition to all of the health benefits of a typical green juice, this juice also delivers the powerful cleansing ability of beet that aids the body in purging toxins and enhancing the health of organs like the kidney and liver.

# Tangerine Takeoff

Two large oranges (peeled)
Three large stalks of celery
One medium sized apple
Two medium sized tangerines
Two medium sized pears
One yam (sweet potato)

This juice not only tastes great, it also has some impressive health benefits as well as it is high in folate, niacin, riboflavin, and vitamins B-6 and K. The pears are also high in boron which prevents calcium loss and promotes bone health. The pears also contain high levels of anti-oxidants and can fight high blood pressure as well as reduce inflammation.

# Cardio Mission

One large slice of pineapple (chop if needed)
One medium sized apple (any variety you like)
One medium sized tangerine
One large cucumber
Half a lemon, peeled
One thumbnail sized piece of ginger
Half a table spoon of pumpkin pie spice

This juice is so sweet you could have it as a dessert while still
getting all the healthy benefits of juicing with fruit and
vegetables. This juice is consistently a favorite for its great taste,
but it can also improve your the function of your cardiovascular
system. Studies have shown that consuming the juices from
apples and lemons can reduce breathing difficulties, improve
oxygen intake, and even prevent the development of asthma in
children. The ginger in this juice will also aid in reduction of
inflammation which can reduce pain and increase mobility.

# Never a Dull Juice

Two parsnips
Two stalks of asparagus
Seven medium sized carrots
Three large stalks of celery
One lemon, peeled
One thumb-sized piece of ginger

There are lots of great reasons to enjoy parsnip juice as a regular part of your diet. Parsnips contain an exceptionally wide variety of various nutrients, vitamins, and minerals. Parsnips are high in folate, potassium, dietary fiber, and vitamin C.

# American Sundown

Two medium sized peaches
Three cups of strawberries
One half of a lime, peeled
One half of a lemon, peeled
Two large apples

Although this is still a healthy juice, it has a relatively high sugar content due to all the fruits. For this reason this juice can be a nice treat once in awhile, but not something you would want to consumer every day. That said, this juice still has some serious health benefits, such as it's detoxifying ability. Strawberries are high in potassium and promote detoxification. They also aid in regulation of the blood pressure.

# Flying Beneath the Radar

Five large carrots
One medium sized Granny Smith apple
One whole lemon, unpeeled
One medium sized tangerine
One thumbnail sized piece of ginger root
One clove of garlic
Four Brussels sprouts

The lemon in this juice gives a strong citrus flavor that is balanced out by the full, earthy carrot flavor that follows. The flavor is too intense for some, and can be toned down by reducing or excluding the ginger and garlic or by adding another apple.

This juice is rich in pectin and as such is a great way to combat high cholesterol. Pectin is found in both apples and carrots and has been definitively linked to substantial reductions in "LDL" cholesterol, aka "bad" cholesterol. There is also some evidence that ginger and lemon assist with the reduction of elevated cholesterol levels as well. The vitamin C in this juice which comes primarily from the carrots can also help to repair dry skin leaving you with skin that feels healthy and looks youthful.

# Packing Potassium

Two medium sized green apples
One fennel bulb and stem
Two large cucumbers
One cup of cauliflower
One lime, peeled
One half lemon, peeled
Thumb-sized piece of ginger

This is a smooth and flavorful green juice that will delight your tastebuds with a surprising hit of lime and ginger. It is an excellent diuretic juice to use as part of a juice cleanse due to its high water content from the cucumbers. It is also packed full of vitamins, in particular vitamin A and vitamin K, as well as a solid amount of potassium.

# Free Radical Eliminator

Two large oranges
Three medium sized tangerines
Two cups of pineapple
Quarter slice of lemon
Two Brussels sprouts
One pinch of cayenne pepper (stirred in after juicing)

This tasty juice provides all the vitamin C you need for a whole day. It is also a superb anti-cancer juice. The anti-oxidant power of the vitamin C works to rid the body of free radicals while the limioid compound in the oranges has been shown to fight a variety of different cancers including breast cancer, stomach cancer, colon cancer, and skin cancer.

# Veg Mix

Two cups of cauliflower
Two beetroot
Three medium sized carrots
One stalk of celery
One small cucumber (or half of one medium sized cucumber)

This juice is a great way to make sure you are getting your daily
recommended amount of manganese and folate as beetroot is rich
in both. This juice is simple and quick to prepare, with no frills,
no fruit, and nothing sweet about it. It is a good juice for when
you are in a rush or don't have many fruits or vegetables handy,
but don't want to skimp on your vegetable consumption.

# Green, Green, White

Two cups of cauliflower
Two cups of spinach
One handful of parsley
Two medium sized Granny Smith apples
Three leaves of kale

The apples provide a hint of sweetness that will make this green juice a favorite even for people who dislike the taste of kale and spinach. The parsley in this juice will also help to reduce the gas and bloating that some people experience when juicing with raw kale. The spinach is a great intestinal tract cleanser that reduces the buildup of waste and facilitates the body's digestive system working efficiently without any digestive issues. The natural laxative found in apples also promotes regular bowel movements. This juice is also rich in vitamins and minerals that the body needs. For example, a small 15 oz glass of this juice provides an entire day's supply of vitamins C and K, as well as the mineral copper.

# Training Tonic

One cup of spinach
One handful of parsley
Two Roma tomatoes
One small green bell pepper (or half a medium sized green bell pepper)
Two large carrots
Two large stalks of celery
One medium sized cucumber
One medium sized tangerine
One small lime
Salt to taste after juicing

This juice is all about health and weight loss as it is very heavy on the vegetables as opposed to fruit. If you need an energy boost to get you through the day you can't go wrong with this juice as it is rich in both phosphorous and potassium.

This juice is also a great recovery drink after a hard workout. This is due not only to the energy boost the juice delivers, but also due to its ability to reduce inflammation. Spinach is highly alkaline which can help to reduce inflammation. The tomatoes are also rich in inflammation-fighting vitamins and nutrients, many of which are contained in the skin of the tomato.

# Cauliflower Chard

Four chard leaves
Two cups of cauliflower
Four kale leaves
One cucumber
Two celery stalks
One lime, peeled
Half of one lemon, peeled
Three cloves of garlic (or to taste)

Garlic in the juicer isn't for everyone, but those who like it tend to like it a lot! Garlic is highly nutritious, containing lots of maganese, fiber, selenium, calcium, copper, iron, and vitamins B1, B6, and C. Studies have shown garlic consumption can help prevent and cure the common cold. Garlic also works to lower cholesterol and blood pressure, and may aid with the prevention of certain brain diseases like Alzheimer's disease and dementia. This is probably due at least in part to the high antioxidant concentration.

# World Class in a Glass

One cup of cauliflower
One large pomegranate
Two medium sized apples
Two medium sized tangerines
One quarter of a lemon
Thumbnail sized piece of ginger root

Pomegranate's truly are a powerhouse when it comes to nutrients and anti-oxidants. Even by the standards of super foods known for their high anti-oxidant concentration, pomegranate leaves most of them in the dust. There is very little fat in a pomegranate and no cholesterol at all. Pomegranate also contains lots of vitamin B5 that helps the body metabolize the macronutrients you consume, which makes this a great juice for anyone trying to lose some weight.

# Parsley Pear Pounder

Three large carrots
One handful of parsley
One medium sized pear, any variety
Four stalks of celery
Two stalks of asparagus
One medium sized stalk of broccoli
One medium sized cucumber
Two table spoons of extra virgin olive oil (stir in after juicing)

This juice is an easy way to load up on folic acid and histamines
which promote blood flow, improved circulation, and can even
boost the libido! Parsley has also been shown to improve blood
flow which can enhance sexual stimulation.

# Juicing Jamboree

One beetroot
One kiwi
Two large peeled oranges
Two medium sized apples
Three medium sized carrots
Half a lemon, peeled

Moderate, consistent carrot consumption has been shown in
studies to reduce cholesterol level by about 10 percent. High
cholesterol is a leading cause of heart disease, therefore carrot
consumption promotes heart health by reducing your risk of heart
disease. Consuming carrots regularly also reduces your risk of a
heart attack. In fact, some studies show a dramatic decrease in
heart attack risk when carrot consumption is maintained over the
course of a year. Drinking this juice daily will could lower your
risk of a heart attack by up to two thirds!

# Gearing Up

Two Roma Tomatoes
One medium sized yellow bell pepper
Two cups of spinach
Two medium sized green apples
Three medium sized carrots
One cup of blueberries
Two large celery stalks

This is a great juice for boosting your immune system, lowering your blood pressure, and losing weight. The high levels of potassium and magnesium in this juice, as well as the two cups of spinach, work together to lower elevated blood pressure. The juice from the green bell pepper contains powerful antioxidants that contribute to a reduction in cholesterol.

# Game On

Six leaves of kale
One cup of broccoli florets
Half a medium sized cucumber
Three medium sized apples, any variety
One medium sized pear, any variety
Two cups of spinach
One lemon

A delicious, Kale based juice that is excellent for weight loss! Kale is considered a "super food" and is ideal for weight loss due to its high concentration of nutrients and low calorie content. It is among the most nutrient-dense vegetables available and this juice makes sure you can easily consume this amazing vegetable daily. Kale is also a significant source of organo-sulfur compounds. Studies show these compounds are effective at fighting many different types of cancer. One of the many amazing qualities of kale is that it can actually contribute to a destruction of cancer cells within the body.

In addition to fighting cancer that already exists in the body, kale has also been shown to prevent cancer from occurring in the first place. The sulforaphane contents of kale has been shown to reduce the risk of cancer from occurring in the body.

In addition to the cancer fighting and preventing power of kale, this drink also contains spinach, which is another vegetable studies have shown to be effective in fighting and preventing various types of cancer. The powerful anti-oxidants contained in this vegetable contribute to the deceleration of cancerous cell production and division.

# Broccoli Apple Aid

Two cups of broccoli florets
One quarter of a small head of green cabbage
Two medium sized Granny Smith apples
One cup of spinach
One thumb sized piece of ginger root
Four medium sized carrots
One lemon, peeled

This juice helps sooth any digestive issues you may be experiencing. The natural laxative in apples can aid with constipation and promote regular bowel movements. The carrots work to cleanse the liver while stimulating a release of bile that is a key component of proper digestions. Juicing with lemon and ginger root not only adds a kick to the juice's flavor, but they also both aid in digestion by reducing gas buildup. Finally, the spinach works to cleanse the intestinal tract while promoting proper digestion.

# The Fast Berry Fill Up

One large pomegranate
One cup of raspberries
One cup of blueberries
One medium sized tangerine
One quarter of a lemon, peeled

This juice is another tasty anti-oxidant powerhouse like the Pomegranate Power recipe also found in this book. Here the sugar content is increased due to the berries which means this is not such a great weight loss juice. It is however a great source of iron, calcium, zinc, magnesium and phosphorus. The delicious sweet taste of this juice makes it an excellent dessert. You can have a sweet treat while avoiding the many other unhealthy foods typically consumed as dessert.

# Delicious Detox

One cup of cauliflower
Two cups of strawberries
Ten leaves of peppermint
Two large apples
One medium sized clementine
Half a lemon

This refreshing juice packs a full day's supply of vitamin C. It also has detoxifying power due to the high potassium content of the strawberries which also helps to regulate blood pressure. In addition to these benefits, strawberries are great for your mental health. Studies have shown that the folic acid found in strawberries facilitates enhanced cognition, memory, and focus. For this reason, this juice would be a perfect choice for studying or working on something that requires prolonged mental focus.

# Liver Liven Up

Three large leaves of red cabbage
One cup of broccoli florets
One beetroot
One large stalk of celery
Three medium carrots
One large orange
One quarter of a pineapple
Three handfuls of spinach
Half a lemon, peeled

The pineapple flavor in this juice helps to even out the earthiness of the beetroot. If it taste too much of beet or cabbage, you can always add some extra pineapple. However you juice it though, this recipe is extremely healthy as it is jam-packed with the vitamins and minerals your body needs.

This juice is a powerful cleanser. The beet juice aids in reducing liver toxicity and combats conditions relating to bile, such as food poisoning, jaundice, hepatitis, diarrhea, and vomiting. The spinach also aids in cleansing the body, especially the intestinal tract, while its high levels of iron help to fortify the blood.

# Tub Scrubber

Five large stalks of celery
Two cups of cauliflower
Two medium sized Granny Smith apples
One medium sized cucumber
Two handfuls of spinach
Five leaves of kale
One quarter of a lemon, peeled
One half of a lime, peeled

They don't come much greener then this tasty, healthy recipe. This juice is a solid choice for anyone wanting to focus on cleansing the body of toxins. Cleansing can be an effective way to jump start a recovery after a binge on unhealthy food or toxic substances like alcohol. It can also be a great way to energize the body even when you normally eat well and live an active lifestyle. If you are doing a juice cleanse, make this drink a staple of the cleanse by drinking it either daily or every other day.

# Night-vision

Two pears
One cup of broccoli florets
One apple, any variety
One honeydew melon, chopped
Two handfuls of red grapes
Two Brussels sprouts

Not only do honeydew melons taste great and yield lots of juice, but they are also a great source of carotenoids. Carotenoids has been shown to promote a variety of desirable health benefits including decreasing the risk of particular cancers and eye diseases. They also have protective benefits for the skin that will help you look and feel younger. Reproductive health and bone density can also improve with regular consumption of carotenoids. The grapes in this juice add a nice, complementary flavor to the melon and more than that, they also contain a variety of anti-inflammatory nutrients that promote longevity!

# The Ballad of Broccoli

Three cups of broccoli florets
Two medium sized apples, any variety
Two beetroot
Three large carrots
One third of a medium sized pineapple

There are lots of great reasons to include beets in your diet. First of all, it is rich in key minerals like potassium, magnesium, and iron. It also packs in high levels of vitamins A, B6 and C. In addition, it is rich in anti-oxidants and low in calories. Unfortunately, not everyone enjoys the taste of beetroot due to its distinct "earthy" flavor. If you are one of those people who wants to consume more beets but you just can't stand the taste, this may be the juice that solves your problem! The apple and the pineapple provide enough of a sweet flavor that the taste of beet is toned down greatly. If you find it is two sweet, you can reduce the quantity of pineapple and include some celery or cucumber instead.

# We would love to hear from you!

We really hope you've been enjoying the recipes in our book and that they've helped you to energize and reach your health and weight loss goals. We'd love to hear from you! If you enjoyed reading this book we would be extremely grateful if you could take just a minute or two of your time and write a review online on Amazon or on social media. We personally read all reviews and they help us to make our future books even better. Thank you so much for your support, it means the world to us!

Yours,
Albert Pino and Fat Loss Frankie

Made in the USA
San Bernardino, CA
21 November 2018